Collins

KS3
Spelling, Punctuation & Grammar

Revision Guide

Paul Burns

About this Revision & Practice book

When it comes to getting the best results, practice really does make perfect!

Experts have proved that repeatedly testing yourself on a topic is far more effective than re-reading information over and over again. And, to be as effective as possible, you should space out the practice test sessions over time.

This revision guide and workbook is specially designed to support this approach to revision and includes seven different opportunities to test yourself on spelling, punctuation and grammar, spaced out over time.

Revise

These pages provide a recap of everything you need to know for each topic.

You should read through all the information before taking the Quick Test at the end. This will test whether you can recall the key facts.

> **Quick Test**
> 1. Is a prefix placed before or after the root word?
> 2. Which letter is always doubled before the addition of a suffix beginning with a vowel?
> 3. What part of speech (word class) is formed by the addition of 'ment' or 'ness'?

Practise

These topic-based questions appear shortly after the revision pages for each topic and will test whether you have understood the topic. If you get any of the questions wrong, make sure you read the correct answer carefully.

Review

These topic-based questions appear later in the book, allowing you to revisit the topic and test how well you have remembered the information. If you get any of the questions wrong, make sure you read the correct answer carefully.

Mix it Up

These pages feature a mix of questions for all the different topics, just like you would get in a test. They will make sure you can recall the relevant information to answer a question without being told which topic it relates to.

Test Yourself on the Go

Visit our website at **collins.co.uk/collinsks3revision** and print off a set of flashcards. These pocket-sized cards feature questions and answers so that you can test yourself on all the key facts anytime and anywhere. You will also find lots more information about the advantages of spaced practice and how to plan for it.

Workbook

This section features even more topic-based questions as well as six 10-minute tests, providing two further practice opportunities to guarantee the best results.

ebook

To access the ebook visit **collins.co.uk/ebooks** and follow the step-by-step instructions.

Contents

	Revise	Practise	Review
Key concepts from KS2			p. 4

Spelling and Vocabulary

	Revise	Practise	Review
Vowels	p. 6	p. 14	p. 26
Homophones	p. 8	p. 14	p. 26
Forming Plurals	p. 10	p. 15	p. 27
Prefixes and Suffixes	p. 12	p. 15	p. 27
Spelling Strategies	p. 16	p. 24	p. 38
Complex and Irregular Words	p. 18	p. 24	p. 38
Extending Your Vocabulary	p. 20	p. 24	p. 38
Using Your Vocabulary Creatively	p. 22	p. 25	p. 39

Punctuation

	Revise	Practise	Review
Ending Sentences	p. 28	p. 36	p. 50
Commas	p. 30	p. 36	p. 50
Colons, Semicolons, Hyphens and Slashes	p. 32	p. 37	p. 51
Parenthesis and Ellipsis	p. 34	p. 37	p. 51
The Apostrophe for Omission	p. 40	p. 48	p. 62
The Apostrophe for Possession	p. 42	p. 48	p. 62
Inverted Commas 1: Quotation and Titles	p. 44	p. 49	p. 62
Inverted Commas 2: Punctuating Speech	p. 46	p. 49	p. 62

Grammar

	Revise	Practise	Review
Nouns	p. 52	p. 60	p. 74
Pronouns	p. 54	p. 60	p. 74
Adjectives and Determiners	p. 56	p. 61	p. 74
Conjunctions	p. 58	p. 61	p. 75
Verbs 1: Tenses	p. 64	p. 72	p. 86
Verbs 2	p. 66	p. 72	p. 86
Adverbs	p. 68	p. 73	p. 87
Prepositions and Interjections	p. 70	p. 73	p. 87
Sentence Structure 1	p. 76	p. 84	p. 88
Sentence Structure 2	p. 78	p. 84	p. 88
Text Structure: Paragraphs	p. 80	p. 85	p. 89
Standard English	p. 82	p. 85	p. 89

Mixed Test-Style Questions p. 90
Answers p. 103
Glossary p. 108
Index p. 112

Key Stage 2 — Review Questions

Spelling

1 Choose the correctly spelt word and insert it in the sentence.

a) If you put the correct ___Answer___, you will get a mark. (asnwer / answer / answere)

b) When I'm older I want to be rich and ___famous___. (famous / famos / famouss)

c) I borrowed two books from the ___library___. (library / libery / librery)

d) It will only take a ___minute___. (minit / minuet / minute)

e) The battle took place in the ___rain___ of George III. (rain / rein / reign) [5]

Vocabulary

1 Which word is a synonym of **peculiar**?

The design of the house was very **peculiar**.

beautiful ☐   regular ☑   odd ☐   unique ☐   [1]

2 Which word is an antonym of **sufficient**?

There was **sufficient** food for everyone.

enough ☐   insufficient ☑   unsufficeint ☐   loads ☐   [1]

3 Add the correct suffixes to the following words to make new words. Choose from:

-ment   -ness   -ful

harsh ___ness/ful___   abandon ___ment___   harm ___ness___   [3]

Punctuation

1 Tick the sentence that must end with a question mark.

He slept for eight hours ☐   Did you get there in time ☐

She wanted to know when the train left ☐   I wonder when we'll arrive ☐   [1]

2 Insert **two** commas in the correct places in the following sentence.

Jo who is my cousin lives in the next road. [2]

3 Insert **two** semicolons in the correct places.

The birds were singing the grass was green the sun was in the sky. [2]

Review

4 Add **two** commas in the correct places.

He bought three apples four oranges a bunch of grapes and a banana. [2]

5 Insert **two** apostrophes in the correct places.

Peters parents live in Paris. Peters in Pimlico. [2]

Grammar

1 Underline the correct word from each pair so that the sentence is in Standard English.

We **done / did** really **well / good** when we sat **them / those** tests. [3]

2 Which **two** of the following four sentences use tense correctly?

After she had done the shopping, she went home. ☐

After she had done the shopping, she goes home. ☐

She went home after she does the shopping. ☐

She did the shopping before she went home. ☐ [2]

3 Rewrite the following sentence in the simple past.

I am baking bread and I really enjoy it. [2]

_____

4 Underline the main verb in the following sentence.

Seeing my friend in the street, I stopped for a chat. [1]

5 The following sentence includes a noun, a verb, an adjective and an adverb. Identify each one.

We sang the beautiful song enthusiastically.

Noun _____   Verb _____

Adjective _____   Adverb _____ [4]

6 Underline the conjunction in the following sentence.

We left early because we had another appointment. [1]

7 Underline the modal verb in the following sentence.

They said they would like to leave early. [1]

Spelling

Vowels

You must be able to:
- Understand how long vowel sounds are spelt
- Understand and use the 'i before e except after c' rule.

Long Vowel Sounds

- One of the first spelling 'rules' you learned was probably that when there is an 'e' at the end of a short word it 'makes the **vowel** say its name', e.g. tame, fine, tone. This is the most straightforward way of spelling words with long vowel sounds.
- A **diphthong** (or blend) is a combination of two sounds – usually vowels that are next to each other – to make a long vowel sound.
- There is no rule about which letters to use for which sound, so you need to look at patterns and learn any spellings you are unsure of.

Long Vowel Sound	Examples
The long 'o' as in 'moon'	soon, macaroon, monsoon blue (the colour), rue, argue blew (past tense of 'blow'), crew, knew, new, through
The long 'o' sound as in 'so'	mow, sow, flow, blow, shown moan, loan, load sew (as in needlework) tone, cone, telephone
The 'ow' sound as in 'loud'	brown, now, cow, fowl (as in chicken) proud, foul (as in bad)
The 'au' sound as in 'caught'	taut (tight), taught (past tense of 'teach') court, sought, bought, brought
The long 'i' as in 'light' (some accents pronounce as 'oi')	light, bright, fight, sight (the ability to see) write, kite, site (a place), cite (refer to) height
The long 'a' as in 'pay'	pray, delay, stay main, stain, remain, attain bane, wane, arcane weight, sleigh, neighbour
The 'oi' sound as in 'loin'	point, anoint, appoint joy, toy, alloy
The 'ai' sound as in 'fair'	lair, pair care, rare, share / tear (as in 'rip')
The long 'u' as in 'sure'	pure, lure, ensure

> **Key Point**
>
> The sound you make might vary according to your **accent** – examples below use '**received pronunciation**' but you may pronounce some of these words differently.

> **Key Point**
>
> If you are unsure of any of these spellings, it might help to put them together in a rhyming **phrase** like 'how now, brown cow', 'the rain in Spain', or 'can the sleigh take the weight of my neighbour?'.

The Rule 'i Before e Except After c'

- This should be one of the best-known and easiest to remember spelling rules – 'i before e except after c'. However, it is important to remember that it applies only when the sound made by the two vowels together is 'ee'.

Examples of 'i' before 'e'		Examples of 'except after c'	
– brief	– belief / believe	– ceiling	– perceive
– tier (as in 'level')	– achieve / achievement	– receive / receipt	– conceive
– thief / thieve	– niece	– deceive / deceit	– conceit / conceited
– chief / handkerchief	– siege / besiege		
– grief / grieve	– reprieve		
– relief / relieve			

Exceptions to the Rule

- Most words commonly thought to be exceptions to the rule are not exceptions if you remember that the rule applies only to words where 'ie' or 'ei' is pronounced as 'ee'. These exceptions include: foreign, their, neighbour ('ei' pronounced 'ay'), forfeit (pronounced as 'i') and albeit ('e' and 'i' pronounced separately).
- Words with 'ie' after 'c' include: efficient, sufficient, ancient and conscience. In all of these, the 'c' and 'i' combine to make a 'sh' sound.
- The only common words that could really be called exceptions are 'weird' (easy to remember because it's a weird spelling) and seize (which you will just have to remember!).

Other Ways of Making 'ee' Sounds

- The most common way of making an 'ee' sound is, of course, 'ee'. Examples include: knee, fee, see, tee, seed, weed, reed, beef, beet, meet, cheese, sneeze, weep and wheeze.
- Another way is to use 'ea'. Examples are: sea, tea, lead, beat, read, knead, please, lease, cease and read.
- Notice that there are a few homophones (words that sound the same – see pages 8–9) in the above lists: tee / tea; see / sea; reed / read; need / knead; beet / beat.

Key Point

When 'i' and 'e' together make an 'ee' sound, the rule is 'i before e except after c'.

Key Point

Long vowel sounds are formed in various ways. The same sound can be spelt in several different ways.

Quick Test

1. What letter at the end of a word makes the preceding vowel 'say its name'?
2. What is an alternative name for a diphthong?
3. a) The rule is 'i' before 'e' except after what?
   b) What sound must the letters 'ie' or 'ei' make for the rule to apply?

Key Words

accent
diphthong
phrase
received pronunciation
vowel

Homophones

You must be able to:
- Understand how two or more words that sound the same can be spelt differently
- Spell these words correctly.

Homophones

- **Homophones** are words that sound the same but have different meanings. Some examples have already been given on pages 6–7.
- Confusing homophones can cause spelling mistakes.
- Sometimes it is possible to come up with a trick or **strategy** to distinguish between homophones. Sometimes you just have to learn them.

Word 1	Meaning	Word 2	Meaning	Way to remember
flu	short for influenza	flew	past tense of 'fly'	Same ending as 'blew' to form the past tense.
through	between	threw	past tense of 'throw'	Same ending as 'flew' and 'blew'.
no	opposite of 'yes'	know	present tense of 'know'	Sound the 'silent k' – 'I **k**now that **K**en has **k**nobbly **k**nees'.
new	recent	knew	past tense of 'knew'	As above.
seen	past participle of 'see'	scene	a view or part of a play	For 'seen' just add 'n' to 'see'.
need	require	knead	what you do with dough	**Knead** the br**ead** on your **k**n**ees**.
hear	listen	here	in this place	You h**ear** with your **ear**s.
heard	past tense of 'hear'	herd	group of animals	Just add 'd' to 'hear'.
way	path	weigh	measure heaviness	It w**eigh**s **eigh**t kilos.
slay	kill	sleigh	mode of transport for the snow	The r**eigh**ndeers n**eigh** when they pull the sl**eigh**.
past	time before now	passed	past tense of 'pass'	To form a past tense you normally add 'ed'.
practise (verb)	rehearse	practice (noun)	the act of practising	Think of advice (noun) and advise (verb) (not homophones).
allowed	let – past tense of 'allow'	aloud	able to be heard	For the first, add 'ed' to form the past. For the second, add 'a' before 'loud'.
whether	'whether or not'	weather	rain, snow, wind, etc.	
serial	something done in instalments	cereal	a crop / breakfast food	'Serial' comes from 'series'. 'Cereal' is from Ceres, goddess of crops.

Revise

- Two of the most frequent confusions are:

| it's | short for 'it is' | its | belonging to it |
| who's | short for 'who is' | whose | belonging to whom |

In both 'it's' and 'who's', the apostrophe denotes **omission** (the leaving out of a letter).

'Whose' and 'its' denote possession but do not require **apostrophes**. When deciding how to spell 'its', think of 'his'.

- Some homophones have more than two meanings and spellings.

Word 1	Meaning	Word 2	Meaning	Word 3	Meaning	Word 4	Meaning
sight	a sense	site	a place	cite	refer to		
to	preposition indicating direction	too	excessive	two	a number		
right	correct	rite	ceremony	write	as in 'write a letter'	wright	someone who makes something

Commonly Confused Words that are Sometimes Homophones

- These words are among the most easily confused. Whether they are homophones or not depends on your accent. For this reason, people from some parts of the country have more trouble with them than people from other parts.

Word 1	Word 2	Word 3	Word 4
there	they're	their	
where	we're	wear	ware
your	you're	yore	

'Our' (meaning 'belonging to us') is an oddity. For some people it's a homophone for 'are'. Others pronounce it like 'hour'. In some accents 'er', 'air', 'ur' and sometimes 'are' sound the same; so, for example, 'fur' (animal hair) and 'fair' (just) are homophones, as are 'care' and 'cur'.

Key Point

Homophones are words that sound the same as each other. They cause a lot of spelling mistakes and confusion about meaning.

Key Point

Whether words are homophones or not sometimes depends on your accent.

Quick Test

1. Why do homophones sometimes make spelling difficult?
2. How might the place where you live influence whether you think words are homophones or not?
3. Are 'advice' and 'practice' nouns or verbs?

Key Words

apostrophe
homophone
omission
strategy

Spelling

Forming Plurals

You must be able to:
- Form plurals from words ending in 'y'
- Form plurals for other irregular words.

Words Ending in 'y'

- When you change words from **singular** to **plural**, you usually add 's'.
- However, sometimes plurals are formed in a different way.
- If the last letter before the 'y' is a vowel, you simply add 's'.
- If the last letter before 'y' is a **consonant**, you change the 'y' to 'ie' and add 's'.

Vowel Comes Before the 'y'

Singular	Plural
bay	bays
quay	quays
key	keys

Change the 'y' to 'ie' and Add 's'

Singular	Plural
baby	babies
berry	berries
cemetery	cemeteries

- This rule also applies when you add 's' to a verb ending in 'y' and often when you form a past tense by adding 'ed' to a verb ending in 'y' – but watch out for **irregular** forms.

Without 's'	With 's'	With 'ed'
allay	allays	allayed
buy	buys	bought
cry	cries	cried

- The rule does not apply to **proper nouns** that end in 'y' – for example when you write about members of the same family. For these, you always just add an 's', e.g. the Johnsons.

Words Ending in 'o'

- There are two different ways to form plurals.
- For some words you just add an 's'. These include all words that end in two vowels (e.g. 'io', 'oo' or 'eo') and musical words. For all other words you add 'es'.

Adding an 's'

Singular	Plural
kangaroo	kangaroos
patio	patios
video	videos

Adding 'es'

Singular	Plural
hero	heroes
potato	potatoes
volcano	volcanoes

 Key Point

There are a few exceptions to this rule. The one you are most likely to use is 'soliloquy', which becomes 'soliloquies' in the plural.

 Key Point

If a word ends in a vowel followed by 'y', just add 's'. If it ends in a consonant followed by 'i', change the 'y' to 'i' and add 'es'.

- What you must **never** do when forming a plural is insert an apostrophe before the 's'.

Other Plurals Ending in 'es'

- Another group of words which add 'es' to make plurals are sometimes known as hissing, buzzing and whooshing words. They include words that end in two or three consonants or 's' or 'x', e.g. bus → buses, flash → flashes, fox → foxes.
- As with the 'i to ies' rule, this also applies to verbs, e.g. crunch → crunches, miss → misses.
- Words ending in 'ix' sometimes change the 'x' to 'c' before adding 'es', e.g. 'appendix' → 'appendices'. However, 'matrix' can become either 'matrixes' or 'matrices'.
- Words ending in 'sis' change to 'es': 'crisis' → 'crises'.
- 'Quiz' doubles the 'z' before adding 'es' to make 'quizzes'.

Irregular Plurals

- Here are some words that form plurals without adding 's' or 'es'. Some plurals retain the Old English (or Anglo Saxon) way of making a plural by using 'en', e.g. child → children, woman → women.
- Some words stay the same in the plural, e.g. aircraft, fish, offspring, sheep.
- In a few words, the vowels change, e.g. foot → feet, tooth → teeth, goose → geese.
- Words ending in 'f' or 'fe' sometimes change the 'f' to 'v' before 's' or 'es' is added, but sometimes the 'f' stays. A small number of words can be made plural either way. For example, life → lives, wolf → wolves, scarf → scarfs / scarves.
- Some of the words which end in 'a', 'um', 'on' or 'us', if taken from Latin or Greek, use classical forms (um → a, us → i, a → ae).
- Others – for various reasons – follow the normal English rules.
- Increasingly, either form is acceptable for many words.

Singular	Plural
curriculum	curricula
formula	formulae *or* formulas
criterion	criteria
radius	radii *or* radiuses
thesaurus	thesauruses *or* thesauri

Quick Test

1. What is the most common way of forming a plural?
2. How do you form plurals of names ending in 'y'?
3. From which language do plurals ending in 'en' come?

Revise

Key Point

In a few cases it is acceptable to add either 's' or 'es'. For example, 'innuendo' can become either 'innuendos' or 'innuendoes'.

Key Point

Some words add 'es' to form plurals. Others are irregular and do not end in 's'.

Key Words

consonant
irregular
plural
proper noun
singular

Prefixes and Suffixes

You must be able to:
- Understand how prefixes and suffixes affect spelling
- Accurately spell words that include prefixes and suffixes.

Prefixes

- A **prefix** is a letter or group of letters added to the start of a word to change its meaning.
- Prefixes do not change the spelling of the **root word**.

Prefix	Variations	Meaning	Example
a	'an' before a vowel	without	amoral, anarchist
anti	'ant' before 'a' or 'o'	opposite, against	anticlimax, antagonist
in	'ig' before 'n'; 'il' before 'l'; 'im' before 'b', 'm' and 'p'; 'ir' before 'r'	not	inoffensive, ignorant, illogical, imbalance, immeasurable, irrelevant
re	sometimes used with a hyphen	again	restore, re-do

Suffixes

- A **suffix** is a letter or group of letters added to the end of a word to change its meaning.

Adding 'ing', 'ed', 'er', 'en' or 'est'
- If the root word ends in 'e', the final 'e' is dropped before adding the suffix.

Root word	+ en	+ ing	+ ed	+ er
bake		baking	baked	baker
write	written	writing		writer

Note that 'write' and 'bite' add 't' before 'en', shortening the vowel sound.

- Many words double the final consonant when a suffix beginning with a vowel is added. Others do not.
- This can be confusing but there are some rules.
- If the word consists of a single **syllable**, includes a short vowel, and ends in one consonant, the final consonant is doubled.

Root word	+ en	+ ing	+ ed	+ er	+ est
dim		dimming	dimmed	dimmer	dimmest
sad	sadden			sadder	saddest

- If a single-syllable word contains a diphthong, the final consonant is **not** doubled.

KS3 Spelling, Punctuation and Grammar Revision Guide

Revise

Root word	+ en	+ ing	+ ed	+ er
beat	beaten	beating		beater
gloat		gloating	gloated	

- When a word has more than one syllable, the consonant is doubled if the **stress** is on the last syllable. If the stress is on another syllable, do not double the consonant.
- In an exception to the doubling rule, words ending in 'l' **always** double the final consonant, regardless of where the stress lies. Words ending in 'w' or 'y' **never** double the final letter.

Root word	+ ing	+ ed	+ er
com<u>mit</u>	committing	committed	
<u>lis</u>ten	listening	listened	listener
travel	travelling	travelled	traveller
play	playing	played	player

Adding 'sion' or 'tion'
- The suffixes 'sion' and 'tion' are added to change verbs into nouns. Often the root word is changed slightly before 'sion' or 'tion' is added. For example, admit → admission, propel → propulsion, evolve → evolution.

Adding 'ence' or 'ance'
- The suffixes 'ence' and 'ance' also change verbs to nouns. Sometimes changes are made to the spelling of the root word. For example, attend → attendance, occur → occurrence.

Adding 'ment', 'ness' or 'ful'
- Another way of forming a noun from a verb is to add 'ment'. In most cases the spelling of the root word is not changed by this suffix but it can be when the root word ends in 'y' or a vowel. For example, accompany → accompaniment.
- The suffix 'ness' is used to change an **adjective** into a noun. Again, the root word spelling very rarely changes. The only exception is when the adjective ends in 'y'. For example, effective → effectiveness, unearthly → unearthliness.
- A similar rule applies when you add 'ful' to a noun in order to make an adjective.

> **Key Point**
>
> Remember there is only one 'l' in the suffix 'ful', although it has the same meaning as the adjective 'full'. For example, beauty → beautiful, shame → shameful, thought → thoughtful.

> **Key Point**
>
> Suffixes have a variety of functions. They often change the way the root word is spelt.

> **Quick Test**
>
> 1. Is a prefix placed before or after the root word?
> 2. Which letter is always doubled before the addition of a suffix beginning with a vowel?
> 3. What part of speech (word class) is formed by the addition of 'ment' or 'ness'?

> **Key Words**
>
> adjective
> prefix
> root word
> stress
> suffix
> syllable

Practice Questions

Vowels

1 Complete the words in the following sentences using diphthongs.

   a) I c _ _ ght a cold so I had to st _ _ in bed.

   b) My mum br _ _ ght up my lunch on a tr _ _.

   c) S _ _ n afterwards I went d _ _ nst _ _ rs to the front door.

   d) There was a cr _ _ d of people _ _ tside.

   e) They were singing and making a lot of n _ _ se. [10]

2 All the following words should contain an 'ee' sound. Insert 'ie', 'ei', 'ee' or 'ea' as appropriate.

   a) bel _ _ ve   – to think something is true

   b) b _ _ ch   – a sandy place by the sea

   c) b _ _ ch   – a kind of tree

   d) dec _ _ ve   – to lie

   e) rec _ _ pt   – a document showing payment has been made

   f) w _ _ rd   – strange [6]

Homophones

3 Pick the correct word for each sentence.

   a) My parents think that rugby is a _____ game.   (rough / ruff)

   b) He didn't know _____ shoes to choose.   (witch / which)

   c) She _____ the test first time.   (past / passed)

   d) You've worked hard. You can have a _____ now.   (break / brake)

   e) The war took place in the _____ of George III.   (rain / rein / reign) [5]

4 Insert the correctly spelt words using the options given.

   a) your / you're

      I know _____ not going to do _____ homework.

Practise

b) there / they're / their

_____ eating _____ lunches over _____ in the yard.

c) were / we're / wear

_____ not the same as we _____ then. For a start, we _____ better clothes.

d) it's / its

_____ not hers but she painted _____ door. [10]

Forming Plurals

5 Form the plurals of these singular nouns.

Singular	Plural
campus	
cello	
crisis	
deer	
festivity	

Singular	Plural
formula	
graph	
ibex	
icicle	
latch	

[10]

Prefixes and Suffixes

6 Add the suffix to the root word to make a longer word.

Root	Suffix	Word
apprehend	+ sion	
bounty	+ ful	
conclude	+ sion	
encourage	+ ment	
flatter	+ er	
implicate	+ tion	
partake	+ ing	
permit	+ ed	
revel	+ er	
spooky	+ ness	

[10]

Spelling Strategies

You must be able to:
- Learn some strategies for remembering spelling you find difficult
- Use the strategies.

General Strategies

- English spelling can be difficult and sometimes illogical. There are, however, ways of learning spellings which you find difficult.
- A traditional way of learning is learning by 'rote'. This means repeating until you remember. Find the correct spelling of a word that has given you trouble and write it out ten times or more. This might sound like a punishment, but it does work.
- Little and often: make a list of difficult words and spend a few minutes each day learning five of them. If possible, ask someone to test you.
- Keep checking. Whenever you need to use a word you're unsure of or find confusing, look it up. If you know the first few letters you should be able to find it quite easily in a **dictionary**. Eventually, you will get to the point where you don't have to look it up anymore.
- If you are using a computer, you might need to check up on spellcheck. Spellcheck is useful but it is not perfect. For example, it will not correct you if you use 'your' instead of 'you're'. It does not consider the context.
- Trace the letters. Some people find it helpful to trace the letters on their palms while saying the word slowly.
- Vocalise: speak the letters out loud while you write the correct spelling.
- Remember that the most effective strategies for learning are usually the ones that you enjoy doing.

> **Key Point**
>
> Check your spellcheck is on 'UK English'. If it isn't on (and it often isn't because 'US English' is its default setting), it will not correct American spellings such as 'color'. The same applies to online dictionaries. If using one, make sure it's British.

Silent Letters

- **Vocalisation** is especially useful for learning words that contain letters that are not clearly pronounced, known as **silent letters**. It can help you to learn if you pronounce – and stress – the silent letters when you are learning the words, for example:
  - autum-**n**   r-**h**yme   **k**-nuckle   w-**h**ether   bom-**b**
- Long words that include silent letters can be made easier to spell by splitting them up and pronouncing each syllable separately, for example:
  - rasp-berry   spag-hetti   lib-ra-ry   sciss-ors   en-vir-on-ment

Splitting up words into syllables can help you learn long words even when there are no silent letters.

- With some short words that contain silent letters, the silent letter stops being silent when a suffix is added. Thinking about the longer word can help you to spell the shorter one:
  - sign – si**g**nature   resign – resi**g**nation   malign – mali**g**nant
    column – colum**n**ist   solemn – solem**n**ity   autumn – autum**n**al

Mnemonics

- A **mnemonic** (itself a hard word to spell – note the silent 'm'!) is a trick to help you remember things.
- Mnemonics are especially useful for helping with words whose spellings are irregular.
- Different people find different sorts of mnemonic useful. The most useful can be ones you make up yourself.
- Words containing the same silent letter can be grouped and turned into sentences. The sillier these are, the easier they are to remember:
  - Kay knits knickers for knights with knobbly knees.
  - At tea in the castle on the trestle table, we listened to the whistler whistling.
  - Rhona the rheumatic rhinoceros dances a rhythmic rhumba.
  - Gee, there are ghastly ghosts and ghouls in the ghetto.
- A common sort of mnemonic used to help with spelling involves using each letter as the first letter in a word to make a sentence.

because	**b**ig **e**lephants **c**an **a**lways **u**pset **s**mall **e**lephants
rhythm	**r**hythm **h**elps **y**our **t**wo **h**ips **m**ove
ocean	**o**nly **c**ats' **e**yes **a**re **n**arrow

- Other mnemonics focus on the part of the word that usually gives the most trouble, associating it with an easily remembered phrase.

sep**a**rate	there is **a** rat in sep**a**rate
ne**c**e**ss**ary	one **c**ollar, two **s**ocks
emba**rr**a**ss**	double trouble
su**cc**e**ss**ful	double delight
station**a**ry	the c**a**r is station**a**ry in the c**a**r park
station**e**ry	pap**e**r is an item of station**e**ry

Quick Test

1. What does 'learning by rote' mean?
2. How can spellcheck on a computer be unhelpful?
3. Into what can you split long words to make them easier to spell?
4. What are the 'g' in 'gnome' and the 'c' in 'indict' called?
5. Which parts of a word should you focus on when making up a mnemonic?

Revise

Key Point

There are many strategies that can help with your spelling, e.g. making posters; making lists of words with the tricky bits in different colours; mnemonics illustrated by drawings. Try them out and see which are most helpful.

Key Point

Mnemonics can help you to remember tricky or irregular spellings.

Key Words

dictionary
mnemonic
silent letter
vocalisation

Complex and Irregular Words

You must be able to:
- Learn how to spell complex and irregular words
- Learn how to spell words that you will need in other subjects.

Spelling in Exams

- To award a good grade in a writing paper, examiners are looking for generally accurate spelling, including some **complex** and unfamiliar words.
- To award a top grade they want to see a high level of accuracy in spelling, including of ambitious **vocabulary**.

Commonly Misspelt Words

- However, 'a high level of accuracy' does mean hardly any errors, so it is important that you can spell as many complex and irregular words as possible.
- Some of the words people have the most difficulty with have been dealt with in previous pages.
- Below is a list of the sort of words that you might be expected to be able to spell at Key Stage 3 but which often cause problems, not including ones that have been mentioned earlier or which clearly follow one of the rules mentioned.
- It is a good idea to work your way through this list and pick out the ones that give you difficulty. Perhaps you could ask someone to test you on them ten at a time. Make a note of the ones you get wrong.
- Once you have a list of the troublesome words, try to apply a rule or come up with another strategy, such as a mnemonic, to help you to remember them. Then ask to be tested again.

> **Key Point**
>
> The examiners recognise that, under exam pressure and without recourse to a dictionary, even the best spellers will make occasional mistakes.
>
> They do not want you to avoid using adventurous vocabulary because you are afraid of misspelling the odd word.

actually	conscious	fortunately / unfortunately	mischievous	questionnaire
alcohol	consequence	fulfil	occasion / occasional / occasionally	queue
analyse / analysis	daughter	imaginary	outrageous	secondary
appear / disappear	definite / definitely	language	parallel	sincerely
business	development	meanwhile	physical	technology / technological
chronology / chronological	diarrhoea	miscellaneous	possession	texture
conscience	exaggerate	mischief /		Wednesday
	exciting			

18   KS3 Spelling, Punctuation and Grammar Revision Guide

Specialist Words

- You should also be able to spell words that may not be common in everyday life but which are important in certain school subjects, for example:

English
alliteration
apostrophe
dialogue
language
metaphor / metaphorical
onomatopoeia
playwright
simile
soliloquy
tragedy

Design and Technology
carbohydrate
fibre
ingredient
protein
specification

Geography
agriculture / agricultural
desert (not to be confused with 'dessert')
estuary

History
dynasty / dynastic
independence
medieval
renaissance

Mathematics
adjacent
approximate / approximately
axis / axes
metre (a unit of length)
perpendicular
quadrilateral

Religious Education
Buddhism
Christianity
disciple
Judaism
mosque
omniscient / omniscience
synagogue

Science
alkaline
amphibian
apparatus
frequency
laboratory
physics
temperature
thermometer
vertebrate / invertebrate

Alternative Spellings

- There are some words where more than one spelling is acceptable and you will get credit for either spelling.
- Many verbs end in either 'ise' or 'ize'. Some people think one is British and one American. In fact, both are acceptable in UK spelling: realise / realisation *or* realize / realization. However, you should decide which form you prefer and stick to it.
- Sometimes it is acceptable to either keep or drop an 'e' when adding a suffix:
  - likeable *or* likable.
- 'Focus' is an unusual word. Despite the rules about doubling consonants, it is acceptable either to double or not double:
  - focus / focusing / focused *or* focus / focussing / focussed.
- Other examples of alternative spellings are:
  - caster / castor
  - hello / hallo / hullo.

> **Key Point**
>
> You should aim for a high level of accuracy in spelling, including spelling complex and irregular words correctly.

> **Quick Test**
>
> 1. What two adjectives describe the sort of words that need to be spelt correctly to receive top exam grades?
> 2. What sort of words should you focus on learning?
> 3. What suffixes are acceptable alternatives to 'ise' and 'isation'?

> **Key Words**
>
> complex
> vocabulary

Extending Your Vocabulary

You must be able to:
- Use a range of vocabulary
- Use words accurately and precisely.

Vocabulary

- Your vocabulary is the range of words that you use.
- To get good marks in exams you are expected to use 'sophisticated', 'adventurous' and 'ambitious' vocabulary.
- To achieve this, you should try to extend your vocabulary beyond the sort of words you use frequently in your everyday life. Avoid using the same word too often in a piece of writing.

Using a Dictionary and a Thesaurus

- When you are reading you will occasionally come across unfamiliar words. Sometimes you can work out their meaning from their context. However, it is always a good idea to use the dictionary to check the precise meaning of the word.
- A **thesaurus** provides **synonyms** and, sometimes, **antonyms**.
- It is important to remember that synonyms do not necessarily have exactly the same meaning. More often, they mean similar but slightly different things.
- For example, if you look up 'walk' you will find a long list of words including amble, hike, hobble, shuffle and strut. These words are all more precise and more evocative than 'walk' but you have to use the right word for the context.
- 'Pat walked down the street' is a bit dull. 'Pat ambled down the street' and 'Pat strutted down the street' are much better but they have different meanings. Having found the words in your thesaurus, if you are not sure of their precise meaning you should look them up in the dictionary so that the words you choose convey your meaning precisely.
- Thesauri provide more than synonyms. The entry for 'weather' gives a long list of words, none of which can simply be substituted for 'weather' in a sentence. Instead, they are types of weather: heatwave, hurricane, lightning, thunder, tornado.
- Often words are misused because they are confused with other words. Sometimes this is because they are homophones or near-homophones. Sometimes they are similar in other ways. It is important to be able to distinguish between them and use the right word to convey your intended meaning.

 Key Point

It is important to use words accurately to convey your intended meaning. Do not use long or unusual words that you do not fully understand just to 'show off'.

 Key Point

A dictionary tells you what words mean and provides you with the correct spelling.

 Key Point

Thesauri and dictionaries are useful tools in expanding your vocabulary.

 Key Point

Aim to use a range of vocabulary, accurately and appropriately.

Revise

Word 1	Meaning	Word 2	Meaning
accept (verb)	receive	except (preposition)	apart from
affect (verb)	impact / change	effect (noun)	consequence / result
alternate (verb)	take turns	alternative (adjective)	choice / substitute
borrow	take temporarily	lend	give temporarily
bought	past tense of 'buy'	brought	past tense of 'bring'
complement	enhance / enhancement	compliment	praise
continual	frequent	continuous	non-stop
discreet	inconspicuous	discrete	individually distinct
disinterested	impartial	uninterested	not interested / bored
enquiry	question	inquiry	investigation
fewer	not as many (number)	less	not as much (quantity)
imply	state indirectly	infer	deduce
lay (transitive verb)	place in a horizontal position	lie (intransitive)	be in a horizontal position / tell an untruth
lose	mislay	loose	not tight
precede	go before	proceed	go forwards
principal	main / (as a noun) headteacher	principle	belief / value
raise (transitive)	elevate / put up	rise (intransitive)	ascend / go up
role	character / job	roll	list / piece of bread
stationary	not moving	stationery	paper / office supplies

Frequently Misused Words

- Watch out for overused and often misused words, e.g.

Word	Meaning	Misuse	Example of misuse
literally	in fact / actually	for emphasis or to mean 'metaphorically'	My heart was literally in my mouth.
iconic	sacred / symbolic	of some significance / popular	The iconic café in the park is to be demolished.

- These words have become **clichés** as they are overused. Try to avoid clichés.

Quick Test

1. What three adjectives describe the sort of vocabulary that examiners want to see?
2. Which reference book gives you the meanings of words?

Key Words

antonym
cliché
synonym
thesaurus

Using Your Vocabulary Creatively

You must be able to:
- Use the way words sound to improve your writing
- Use words to create images.

Using Sounds

- **Alliteration** can be a very effective tool. It is often used in poetry but also frequently by journalists who want to create snappy and memorable headlines. Alliteration means repeating the same initial sound (not necessarily letter) in a string of words:
  - 'While I nodded, nearly napping' (from 'The Raven' by Edgar Allen Poe)
  - Bright Bertie Beats the Bakers.
- Different consonants can help to create different moods. For example, 'k' and 'g' sounds are harsh sounding (*bang, kick, grind*), while 's' and 'f' are soft and can create a gentle or sad mood:
  - 'Full fathom five thy father lies' (from *The Tempest* by William Shakespeare).
- **Sibilance**, using initial 's' sounds, is a particularly effective form of alliteration:
  - The slimy snake slithered swiftly.
- Repetition can be used to emphasise a thought or feeling:
  - 'Alone, alone, all, all alone' (from 'The Rime of the Ancient Mariner' by Samuel Taylor Coleridge).
- The repetition of vowel sounds within words is called **assonance**. In this example the combination of long 'i' and short 'i' sounds reflects the sharp danger of the storm:
  - 'A still brighter white snake wriggles among it, spilled' (from 'Storm in the Black Forest' by DH Lawrence).
- **Onomatopoeia**, where the sound reflects the meaning of the word, can be used to dramatic effect:
  - The door clanged shut.
  - The fireworks fizzed and crackled in the dark.

> **Key Point**
>
> To use your vocabulary to greatest effect, you should think about how words sound as well as their meaning.

Using Imagery

- **Imagery** is the use of words to create pictures in the reader's mind. The term 'literal imagery' refers to the description of things as they are. 'Figurative imagery' uses the image of one thing to describe something else.
- The simplest form of figurative imagery is the **simile**, which uses 'as' or 'like' to compare the thing being described with something

else, thereby giving a stronger idea of what it is like or how the writer feels about it. Some similes are common sayings: 'hungry like a wolf' or 'as warm as toast'. While these similes can give variety to your writing, an original simile can really enhance it.

- A **metaphor** creates a striking image by implicit comparison, speaking about one thing as if it were the other. Some metaphors are so common in everyday speech that we often don't realise they are metaphors:
  – She's a little angel.   – It's been an uphill battle.
- **Personification** is a kind of metaphor. It means writing about an emotion or idea as if it were a person:
  – Time marches on.   – Mother Nature will take care of that.
- The phrase '**pathetic fallacy**' is used to describe two different but related literary techniques. One is a kind of personification where an aspect of nature is given human qualities:
  – The sun smiled down on us.
  Pathetic fallacy can also mean using a literal description of the weather or landscape to reflect the feelings of the writer or a character. For example, a description of a dull, rainy day might be used to convey a character's sadness.
- **Symbolism** is the use of an object to represent an idea or feeling. Traditionally, a heart is symbolic of love and a lamb of innocence. A great oak tree can be a symbol of strength.

Other Linguistic Techniques

- **Irony** is the use of words stating the opposite of what is meant, or sometimes using understatement, to convey meaning in a witty manner. When spoken (and not very subtle) it is called sarcasm. For the reader to understand irony, its true meaning must be clear from the context:
  – I got two detentions from my old mate the deputy head.
  – He's not the sharpest knife in the drawer.
- **Hyperbole** is another word for exaggeration. Please remember that, as to exaggerate means to overstate, there is no such thing as 'over exaggerating'. Hyperbole is especially useful when expressing strong feelings:
  – My parents will kill me when I get home.
  – I could eat a horse.
- An **oxymoron** is two words which have contradictory meaning put together, often to convey confusing or conflicting feelings:
  – cold fire   – deafening silence

> ### Quick Test
> 1. What is the correct term for the repetition of a sound at the start of a series of words?
> 2. In onomatopoeia, what does the sound of a word resemble?
> 3. Sarcasm is a form of what literary technique?
> 4. Of what technique is 'loving hate' an example?

Key Point
An original metaphor can say a lot more than the literal image it replaces.

Key Point
Think about how words sound as well as what they mean.

Key Point
Using imagery can enhance and improve your creative writing.

Key Words
alliteration
assonance
hyperbole
imagery
irony
metaphor
onomatopoeia
oxymoron
pathetic fallacy
personification
sibilance
simile
symbolism

Practice Questions

Spelling Strategies, and Complex and Irregular Words

1 The following words have been spelt incorrectly. Write down the correct spelling for each.

a) dissappear .... f) jelousie ....

b) exagerrate .... g) mischevious ....

c) fearcely .... h) playwrite ....

d) fizzical .... i) seperate ....

e) independance .... j) sincearly .... [10]

2 Rearrange the letters to give the correctly spelt word.

Letters	Meaning	Answer
ytalluca	in fact	a
reetm	a measurement of length	m
riyad	a book of engagements	d
nosccceeni	sense of right and wrong	c
lapearll	(lines) side by side with the same distance between them	p

[5]

3 The following passage contains **five** spelling mistakes. Find them and write the correct spellings underneath.

Every year in Febuary on my father's birthday we have a big problem. We can never decide what to get him for a present. He does not drink alcohol or eat choclates. People say, 'Get him a book', but unfortunitely he doesn't read much. He says, 'I don't want presents, just your presance', which is extremely corny. This year we got him a gift vowcher.

.... [5]

Extending Your Vocabulary

4 Insert the correct words in the sentences below.

a) bought / brought

In the shop we .... new hats.

We .... our pencil cases to school.

Practise

    b) practice / practise

        If you want to improve you will have to _____.

        I was late for football _____ again.

    c) imply / infer

        I _____ from your expression that you're annoyed.

        Are you trying to _____ I've done something wrong?

    d) affect / effect

        I try not to let the weather _____ me.

        The rain has no _____ on my mood.

    e) lay / lie

        Will you _____ the table please?

        I need to _____ down. [5]

5 In the following passage, **five** words are used incorrectly. Find them and write the correct words underneath.

I would not normally burrow money from anyone, as a matter of principal. However, yesterday in the dinner cue I realised I had less than a pound on me so I could not pay for my meal. Luckily Sam was next to me and she asked very discretely if I would like some money. I excepted her offer.

_____   _____   _____   _____   _____ [5]

Using Your Vocabulary Creatively

6 Of which linguistic techniques are the following examples? Choose from:

        alliteration   assonance   hyperbole   metaphor   simile

    a) As quiet as a mouse, I hid from the giant but I was shaking like a leaf. _____

    b) Dashing Dan and his dog Dilly dive daringly. _____

    c) It means the world to me. I'm a hundred and ten per cent committed. _____

    d) How profound the clown seems now. _____

    e) You are my rock. _____ [5]

Review Questions

Vowels and Homophones

1 Insert the correctly spelt words in the following pairs of sentences.

   a) mite / might

      She felt sorry for the little _____.

      He _____ go to the concert. He hasn't decided yet.

   b) made / maid

      In the 19th century, many large households had a _____.

      She _____ the beds every morning.

   c) aloud / allowed

      Would you like me to read _____?

      Eating is not _____ in the classroom. [3]

2 Insert **their**, **there**, **they're**, **wear**, **were**, **we're**, **where**, **your** or **you're** into the following sentences so that they make sense. One word is used twice.

   a) _____ are you going?

   b) I've met them before but I can't remember _____ names.

   c) John and I can't come to the party because _____ in Florida.

   d) If you want to find it, look over _____.

   e) If you _____ that, you'll look ridiculous.

   f) I counted them and _____ are ten altogether.

   g) I think you should ask _____ mother before you decide.

   h) _____ not here. I don't know where I put them.

   i) They _____ definitely on the table yesterday.

   j) I'm glad _____ here so I can explain it all to you. [10]

Review

Forming Plurals

3 Form the plurals of these singular nouns.

Singular	Plural
Parry (name)	(the)
pass	
ploy	
raspberry	
rush	

Singular	Plural
sheaf	
ski	
turkey	
veto	
zoo	

[10]

Prefixes and Suffixes

4 Add 'ing' to the following words to form a correctly spelt word.

a) age ....

b) omit ....

c) regret ....

d) neglect ....

e) hesitate ....

f) monitor ....

[6]

5 Add the prefix 'anti', 'ig', 'il', 'im', 'in', 'ir' or 'un' to each of the following adjectives to form a correctly spelt word.

a) equal ....

b) offensive ....

c) perfect ....

d) legible ....

e) defeated ....

f) defensible ....

g) noble ....

h) social ....

i) capable ....

j) resistible ....

[10]

6 The following paragraph contains **ten** incorrect spellings. Underline them and then write the correct spellings below.

Becos we could not go away on holiday during the summer brake, we decided to go for a long walk every day. Usually we walked in the park but ocassionally we went down to the river or just wondered around the streets. Sometimes we walked for up to eight kilometers, just looking around us as we walked passed houses, shops, churchs and cinemas. I know it doesn't sound very exiting but it past the time and did us a lot of good. I certainly lost a lot of wait!

....

....

....

[10]

Punctuation

Ending Sentences

You must be able to:

- Understand how to use punctuation to end a sentence
- Use full stops, question marks and exclamation marks correctly and effectively.

Full Stops

- A full stop (.) is the most basic means of punctuating your writing. It is the usual way of ending a sentence.
- A sentence is a group of words that forms a statement, command, question or exclamation and makes sense on its own.
- If a sentence is a statement, it always ends with a full stop. A command can end with a **full stop** or an **exclamation mark**.
- A sentence always has a main **clause**. A clause is a group of words that contains a **subject** and a **predicate**. A group of words that does not contain both of these is called a phrase.
- Sentences can consist of more than one clause (see pages 76–79).
- The subject is the person or thing that the sentence is about, usually the person or thing performing an action but sometimes (with a passive verb) the person or thing having something done to him / her / it. The subject comes at the beginning of the clause:
  - <u>Miriam</u> explained how the process would work.
  - <u>The horse</u> was brushed by the groom.

- The predicate is the rest of the clause. It includes the verb and gives information about the subject:
  - Miriam <u>explained how the process would work.</u>
  - The horse <u>was brushed by the groom.</u>

In the first example, the verb is 'explained' and in the second sentence, it is 'was brushed'.

- Sometimes, for effect (usually in creative writing), you might deliberately use a full stop to end a **fragment**, which is not strictly a sentence:
  - Then I saw it. The gun.

The second 'sentence' has a subject but no predicate.

- Commands do not always include a subject. The subject is implied:
  - Get on with your work.

The implied subject is the person or people being given the command or instruction.

- Full stops are important because they mark the end of one statement or thought and make you pause before you begin the next sentence, whose beginning is marked by the use of a capital letter.
- If you do not include full stops, your writing will be virtually impossible to understand.
- Probably the most common punctuation error is the use of **commas** instead of full stops to divide clauses. This is called **comma splicing**, for example:
  - She walked to the café, she ate an ice cream. ✗
  - She walked to the café. She ate an ice cream. ✓

There are several ways in which you can turn these two separate short sentences into one longer one. These are dealt with in the section on sentences (pages 76–79).

Initials and Abbreviations

- Full stops are sometimes used when names or titles are shortened to initials or long words are shortened:

    J.K. Rowling   B.B.C.   admin.

    However, this is becoming less common and it is acceptable to omit the full stop:

    JK Rowling   BBC   admin

Question Marks

- A **question mark** (?) is used to show that a sentence is a question.
- It is used only for direct questions:
  - Are you eating?
- It is not used in indirect speech or when a question is implied:
  - He asked her what she wanted to eat.
  - I wonder whether it would taste nice.
- A question mark is used to end a **rhetorical question**. These are often used in speeches and journalism. A rhetorical question is a linguistic device which does not expect the listener or reader to give an answer. It is designed to make you think about the question. Often the expected answer is implied:
  - Is this the sort of future we want for our children?

Exclamation Marks

- An exclamation is a sudden remark or cry, expressing pain, surprise or strong emotion. It is followed by an exclamation mark (!).
- Usually exclamations are complete sentences:
  - I don't believe it!
- They can be fragments:
  - What a surprise!
  - Ouch!
- Inexperienced writers tend to overuse exclamation marks. They are especially common in text messages, possibly because it is difficult to express emotion in a short message that lacks context. Use them sparingly in your writing.

> **Quick Test**
>
> 1. Which punctuation mark is used to end a statement?
> 2. Which two punctuation marks can end a command?
> 3. How should you begin a new sentence?
> 4. What is the use of commas instead of full stops called?
> 5. What does an exclamation express?

Revise

 Key Point

A sentence can be ended by a full stop, a question mark or an exclamation mark.

The main verb asks a question by changing the position of the subject. 'You are eating' is a statement.

These sentences are statements, not questions, because the main verbs state what the subject is doing. Therefore, they end with full stops.

 Key Point

Question marks should only be used to indicate direct questions.

 Key Words

clause
comma
comma splicing
exclamation mark
fragment
full stop
predicate
question mark
rhetorical question
subject

Ending Sentences: Revise   29

Commas

You must be able to:
- Understand how commas should be used
- Use commas correctly and effectively.

Lists

- Commas are used to separate items in a list.
- The comma is placed after each word or phrase except for the **penultimate** one. That is separated from the last item by a conjunction (either 'and' or 'or'):
  - We bought a hat, a coat, a pair of trousers and two jumpers.
  - You may have apple pie, chocolate cake, meringue or a fruit salad.
- It is not incorrect to put a comma before the conjunction. This is sometimes called the Oxford comma. Usually, it is unnecessary but it can be useful when the items in the list are a little longer, especially if one or more of them includes a conjunction. In such cases the Oxford comma can clarify the meaning:
  - We brought with us a blue and yellow towel, a bat and ball, a bucket and spade, and a tent.
- You can also use commas to separate adjectives before a noun. People do not do this as much as they used to, but it can be helpful, especially if there are more than two adjectives:
  - There in front of us stood a huge, dark, ruined castle.

Separating Clauses and Phrases within a Sentence

- Commas are used to demarcate parts of a sentence that are not part of the main clause and without which the sentence would still make sense.
- **Adverbials**, which can be single words (**adverbs**), phrases (**adverbial phrases**) or clauses (**adverbial clauses**), can be separated from the rest of the sentence using a comma or commas.
  - Actually, I'd rather not go.
  - When she has the time, she goes to see her grandmother.

  In these examples there is no loss of sense if the comma is omitted so it is acceptable not to use one. As with the Oxford comma, there are times when this use of the comma is helpful in making the meaning clear.

- Adverbial phrases and clauses do not usually need a comma if placed at the end of the sentence:
  - I'm going to the cinema after dinner.
  - She goes to see her grandmother when she has the time.
- Commas can be useful if the adverbial is put in the middle of the sentence:
  - She goes, when she has time, to see her grandmother.

  Here the second comma is needed to convey the correct meaning. 'She goes, when she has time to see her grandmother' means something a little different.

- While they must never be used on their own to connect two clauses (comma splicing), commas can be used with a conjunction to connect an adverbial clause to a main clause:
  - Billy was the tallest boy in the class, so he won the high jump.
- When adverbials are used as connectives, connecting a sentence to the previous one, commas should be used to separate them from the main clause:
  - However, I do not agree with the next point you made.
  - I do not, however, agree with the next point you made.
  - As a result, I will not be supporting the motion.
- **Adjectival clauses** are **subordinate clauses** that are introduced by **relative pronouns**, such as 'that', 'which' or 'who'. Whether you use a comma or not depends on the meaning of the sentence:
  - The police officer arrested the boy who had brown hair.
  - The police officer arrested the boy, who had brown hair.

  In the first of these sentences the adjectival clause identifies which boy the police officer arrested (the boy with brown hair – not any of the other boys). In the second example the adjectival clause gives a bit of extra information, which is not essential.
- In the same way, commas can separate **adjectival phrases** from the rest of the sentence:
  - Billy, the tallest boy in the class, won the high jump.

Direct Speech

- Commas are used to introduce **direct speech**:
  - He said, 'Do you find punctuation rather confusing?'

  Note the use of the capital letter at the beginning of the speech although it is not following a full stop.
- Commas are also used to end direct speech:
  - 'Not particularly,' she answered.

  Here the comma is within the **inverted commas**.
- If the 'said' bit interrupts a sentence, a comma introduces the second part of the sentence when speech is resumed.
  - 'I'm glad to hear it,' he replied, 'but I think you should go.'
- Commas are used when someone is addressed directly:
  - 'Children, you can put down your pens now.'

> ### Quick Test
> 1. Is it acceptable to use a comma before 'and' in a list'?
> 2. When is a comma followed by a capital letter?
> 3. Which two of these can follow a comma to join two clauses?
>   **relative pronoun   conjunction   proper noun**
> 4. Which of the following is separated from the main clause by a comma?   **subject   object   subordinate clause**

Revise

Key Point
See pages 76–79 for more about sentence structure.

For more help with punctuating direct speech see pages 46–47.

Key Point
Commas are used to separate items in a list.

Key Point
Commas are used to separate phrases and clauses within a sentence.

Key Words
adjectival clause
adjectival phrase
adverb
adverbial
adverbial clause
adverbial phrase
direct speech
inverted commas
penultimate
relative pronoun
subordinate clause

Commas: Revise

Colons, Semicolons, Hyphens and Slashes

You must be able to:
- Use colons and semicolons correctly and effectively
- Use hyphens and slashes correctly and effectively.

Colons

- **Colons** (:) can add variety to your writing and make your meaning clearer.
- Their function is to introduce something.
- They are used to introduce lists where the things listed are not the direct objects of a verb:
  - We had a go at all the activities: windsurfing, scuba-diving, climbing and abseiling.
- They are used to introduce **quotations**:
  - Mercutio plays down his injury: 'Ay, ay, a scratch, a scratch.'
  Or (for a longer quotation):
  - Juliet expresses her dilemma:
    My only love sprung from my only hate!
- A colon can replace a full stop when two clauses are closely connected and the second clause explains or expands on the first. The colon introduces the explanation or expansion:
  - I love history: learning about the past teaches you about the present.
  These two clauses could also be connected by the conjunction 'because'. Using the colon, however, gives a bit more impact to the statement.

Semicolons

- **Semicolons** (;) are used to separate items in a list. They help to avoid confusion if one or more of the items in the list contains a comma:
  - There was quite a range of people at the party: all my brothers and sisters; the next door neighbours; Carol, who lives across the road; Tony, Carol's husband; and my cousins.
- Semicolons are used to bring together two closely related clauses:
  - Thunder cracked; lightning flashed.
  - I live in number ten; Kara lives in number twelve.
  Here it would be acceptable to have the two clauses as separate sentences, divided by a full stop, but the writer has chosen to use a semicolon in order to connect the two statements.

Key Point

Colons are used to introduce lists. Semicolons are used to separate items in a list.

Key Point

Colons are used to introduce explanatory clauses. Semicolons are used to connect closely related statements.

It would also be acceptable to join the two clauses using a conjunction:
- I live in number ten and Kara lives in number twelve. Leaving out the conjunction can add to the impact of the statements.
- If you wish to connect two statements and show their connection by using an adverb, you can use a semicolon rather than starting a new sentence.
  - I'd like to join you; however, I'm doing my homework.
- Semicolons connect clauses, not phrases. To check you have used a semicolon in the correct way, look at whether the two parts of the sentence could stand alone as sentences.
- Semicolons should be used sparingly and consciously, either to clarify meaning or for effect.

Hyphens

- **Hyphens** (-) are used to connect two or more words to make compound words:
  merry-go-round   three-year-old   heart-to-heart   non-starter
- A lot of **compound words** do not use hyphens:
  heartache   nonconformist
- Some compound words can be formed either way:
  cooperative *or* co-operative

Slashes

- A forward slash (/), sometimes called a **solidus** or a **virgule**, can be used as a substitute for 'or'. Usually it is better to use 'or' in formal writing but there are times when the slash is neater or clearer:
  - Every student should bring his / her own stationery. (This is more elegantly expressed as 'All students should bring their own stationery.')
  - You can have butter and / or cheese on your bread.
- Slashes are also used to separate parts of internet addresses, in fractions and in dates when they are expressed numerically (5/12/21).
- Slashes can be used in a short quotation that runs over two or more lines of poetry, indicating where one line ends and the other begins:
  Tyger tyger, burning bright / In the forests of the night;
  William Blake, 'The Tyger'

Revise

> **Key Point**
>
> There are no hard and fast rules about when words should be hyphenated. 'We had a heart-to-heart' is no better or worse than 'we had a heart to heart'. It is a matter of whether the hyphen makes the meaning clearer and of personal taste.

> **Key Point**
>
> Hyphens are used to link words in order to create new compound words.

> **Quick Test**
>
> 1. What are the four things that a colon can introduce?
> 2. The presence of what in an item suggests semicolons should be used to separate items in a list?
> 3. What kind of word can be used instead of a semicolon: a noun, a conjunction or a preposition?
> 4. What sort of words can be formed with a hyphen?
> 5. What are 'solidus' and 'virgule' alternative terms for?

> **Key Words**
>
> colon
> compound words
> hyphen
> quotation
> semicolon
> solidus
> virgule

Colons, Semicolons, Hyphens and Slashes: Revise   33

Parenthesis and Ellipsis

You must be able to:
- Understand how brackets, dashes and ellipsis should be used
- Use brackets, dashes and ellipsis effectively.

Brackets

- **Brackets** ((…)) are used to put words or phrases in parenthesis. Because of this they are sometimes referred to as **parentheses**. However, **dashes** can also perform this function.
- A **parenthesis** is a word, phrase or clause inserted into a sentence independently of grammatical sequence. This means it does not have to be connected to the rest of a sentence in the same way as a subordinate clause.
- It is helpful to think of parenthesis as the written equivalent of an '**aside**' or 'by the way'.
- Parenthesis enables the writer to add extra information, some explanation or even an observation that is a bit off the subject. It can help to create an informal, chatty tone.
- You can put a whole sentence within brackets:
  - I was disappointed when Mum invited Ron to the party. (He's the one I told you about.)

  Or
  - I was disappointed when Mum invited Ron (he's the one I told you about) to the party.
- It is more usual to put a phrase in brackets:
  - I was disappointed when Mum invited Ron (next-door neighbour, flashy car) to the party.
  - I was disappointed when Mum invited Ron, who is our next-door neighbour and has a flashy car, to the party.
- You can insert a single word into brackets:
  - Mum invited Ron (neighbour) to the party.
- You can use brackets if you want to give an alternative word or establish an abbreviation or initials you intend to use later:
  - The forward slash (solidus) has several different functions.
  - University College, London (UCL) is offering many courses.
- Square brackets ([…]) are used when supplying a word or words that make a quotation clearer, especially if part of the original has been omitted or the original words might cause confusion. The use of square brackets makes it clear that the words within them were not part of the original text:
  - Mrs Gardiner expressed an inclination to see [Pemberley] again.

  Jane Austen, *Pride and Prejudice*

Here the parenthesis is used because putting the extra information into a subordinate clause would take longer and it would lose its impact:

Here 'Pemberley' replaces 'the place' because the reader might not know to which place the writer is referring.

Dashes

- Dashes (–) are traditionally longer than hyphens.
- Dashes are used to indicate parenthesis, in all the same ways as round brackets:
    - I took my best coat – it's the red one – to the cleaner's.
    - I took my best coat – the red one – to the cleaner's.
    - I took my best – red – coat to the cleaner's.
- They can also be used to replace some other punctuation marks.
- They can replace colons.
    - There was only one explanation – murder.
  In this sentence the dash might also indicate a pause for effect, which can also be indicated by ellipsis. A similar effect is created here:
    - I am afraid it was a case of – murder.
- You can also use them to replace semicolons:
    - It was my coat – they weren't my gloves.
- Dashes are also used between numbers, including dates, to indicate a range or length of time.
    - I answered questions 1–14 in no time.
    - Rosa Parks (1913–2005) played an important role in the civil rights movement in America.
- The dash can create an informal or dramatic tone. If it is used too often it can make a text look unattractive or confusing.

Ellipsis

- **Ellipsis** (…) is used to show that one or more words have been omitted from the text. It is used in quotations to show that unimportant or irrelevant words have been left out. Because of this it is especially useful when writing English Literature essays:
    - Elizabeth…was too much oppressed to make any reply.
              Jane Austen, *Pride and Prejudice*
  If you are quoting verse you can use ellipsis to show that your quotation starts part way through a line:
              … 'tis purchased by the weight,
        Which therein works a miracle in nature,
              William Shakespeare, *The Merchant of Venice*
- Ellipsis can also be used to indicate a dramatic pause:
    - 'I will not give house room to this…monstrosity,' he gasped.
- It is sometimes used at the end of a sentence to show a thought trailing off or to leave the reader wondering what might happen next:
    - There were just too many coincidences…

Key Point

Brackets or dashes can be used to put words, phrases or whole sentences in parenthesis.

Key Point

Dashes can be used instead of brackets, colons, semicolons or ellipsis. Their effect can be dramatic or informal.

Key Words

aside
brackets
dash
ellipsis
parenthesis / parentheses

Quick Test

1. For what are parentheses an alternative name?
2. How does a sentence within brackets end?
3. What punctuation marks can you use instead of brackets?

Practice Questions

Ending Sentences

1 Rewrite the paragraph below on a separate piece of paper. Insert full stops and capital letters in the correct places. There should be **ten** sentences.

it is a short walk from town to our house the house is built on the side of a gently sloping hill a blue gate leads to a short gravel path this takes you to the front door it is not a particularly attractive house but it is very welcoming there are two reception rooms and a large kitchen downstairs a door from the kitchen leads out onto the back garden upstairs you will find three bedrooms and a bathroom from my room there is a stunning view of the river my family have lived there for over a hundred years [10]

2 Complete each of the following sentences with a full stop, question mark or exclamation mark.

a) The house belongs to my grandfather

b) Have you lived there long

c) We don't know whether we should move in

d) Gosh, it's beautiful

e) How many rooms are there altogether [5]

Commas

3 Insert either **one** or **two** commas in each of the following sentences so that they make sense.

a) There are three bedrooms a bathroom two reception rooms and a kitchen.

b) Ideally I'd like to have it fully restored.

c) The local shop which is about a mile away doesn't have a wide range of food.

d) There are however a lot more shops in town.

e) 'I wouldn't sell if I were you' she remarked.

f) Old Ben our nearest neighbour will be moving in the spring. [10]

Practise

Colons, Semicolons, Hyphens and Slashes

4 Insert **one** colon and **four** semicolons in the following paragraph so that it makes sense.

My grandparents keep a lot of animals Jemima the horse, who has been with them the longest Dino the Airedale, who came from a local charity a three-legged cat called Fred two guinea pigs without names and, last but not least, ten noisy but useful brown hens. [5]

5 Tick the **five** sentences that are correctly punctuated.

a) Dino was a rescue dog: he had been abandoned by the side of the road. ☐

b) The guinea pigs were very friendly, the cat was unsociable. ☐

c) They had seen a poster in the shop: 'good homes needed for strays'. ☐

d) I'll be visiting them at half-term. ☐

e) Fred / Dino have become great friends. ☐

f) We were worried; about the hens not laying eggs. ☐

g) Sometimes the eggs are brown; at other times they are white. ☐

h) It is usual to bring a card and / or present to a birthday party. ☐

i) The hens-and-geese live in the barn. ☐

j) We like; animals: trees: and flowers. ☐ [5]

Parenthesis and Ellipsis

6 Insert brackets or dashes in the correct places in the following sentences.

a) Gillian the one who likes horses lives in the next village.

b) The Department for Education DfE is in charge of national policy for schools.

c) The guinea pigs Please don't interrupt me, Giles. haven't been fed today.

d) There's only one person responsible for this you.

e) My grandma Mrs Harrsion to you is out at the moment. [5]

Review Questions

Spelling Strategies, and Complex and Irregular Words

1 Tick the **four** words below that are correctly spelt.

a) perpendicular ☐

b) potatos ☐

c) conshious ☐

d) verterbrate ☐

e) amphibian ☐

f) miscellaneous ☐

g) neccesary ☐

h) embarrassment ☐

i) dialog ☐ [4]

2 Complete the incomplete words in the passage below.

You may opt for a general s............e course or choose to study three separate subjects: biology, c............y and p............s. All lessons take place in a l............y. At the end of the course, you will be a............d by practical and written exams. [5]

Extending Your Vocabulary

3 Here are words that can be used instead of 'say'.

announce   exclaim   mention   murmur   retort

Match each one to one of the definitions below.

a) To cry out suddenly ....

b) To reply wittily or angrily ....

c) To speak in a low voice ....

d) To make publicly known ....

e) To refer to briefly .... [5]

Review

4 Insert the correct words in the sentences below.

a) lose / loose

If you _____ this pen, you won't get another one.

The water was spilt because the bottle top was _____.

b) enquiry / inquiry

I don't know when the train leaves so I'll make an _____ at the station.

I have been asked to hold a full _____ into the case.

c) compliment / complement

I'd like to _____ you on your success.

The sauce _____ s the dish perfectly.

d) allude / elude

The answer completely _____ s me.

In the course of the lecture he _____ d to his own book several times.

e) uninterested / disinterested

I didn't go to the talk because I'm completely _____ in butterflies.

I've asked Moira to chair the meeting because she's totally _____. [5]

Using Your Vocabulary Creatively

5 Pick **one** of the words or phrases listed below and insert it into the appropriate sentence to create the specified technique.

    loose cannon   Love   as an ox   angry   sang sweetly

a) She was as strong _____. (simile)

b) _____ conquers all. (personification)

c) The _____ skies darkened above us. (pathetic fallacy)

d) Saira _____ for us. (sibilance)

e) You can't rely on him: he's a bit of a _____. (metaphor) [5]

The Apostrophe for Omission

You must be able to:
- Understand how apostrophes are used to show omission
- Use the apostrophe for omission confidently.

Omission

- Apostrophes (') can be used in two ways: to show possession and to indicate **omission**. Do not use them for any other reason.
- Omission means leaving something out. Use an apostrophe to show when you have omitted a letter or letters from a word.
- Sometimes this usage is referred to as **contraction**. This term is a bit more accurate as it acknowledges that often two or more words are put together when an apostrophe is used.
- Contractions should not normally be used in formal writing.
- Even when writing **dialogue**, you may want to use the full form of words rather than the contraction to create a more formal and forceful tone:
  - 'You must not do that' rather than 'You mustn't do that'.

Informal Negatives
- One of the most common uses of contraction is in informal negatives, when 'not' is added to a verb and the 'o' is omitted:
  - is not → isn't – cannot → can't – should not → shouldn't

The Verb 'to be'
- The present tense of the verb 'to be' is often contracted in speech and informal writing.
- In the singular 'she is', 'he is', 'it is' and 'who is' become 'she's', 'he's' 'it's' and 'who's'. It is important not to confuse 'it's' with 'its' or 'who's' with 'whose'.
- This can be done with nouns as well as **pronouns**:
  - The dog's in the kitchen.
  - Marc's on the phone.
- 'I am' becomes 'I'm' and 'you are' becomes 'you're' by omitting the 'a'.
- In the plural 'we are' is replaced by 'we're', 'you are' by 'you're' and 'they are' by 'they're'. These words are commonly misspelt. However, if you just think about the full form before writing the contracted form, you should have no trouble.
- You cannot use nouns before 're.

Key Point

'Will not' and 'shall not' are treated differently. In both cases more than one letter is missed out and an additional letter inserted:

will not → won't

As normal, the 'o' of not is omitted. 'ill' is omitted from 'will' and replaced by 'o'. This is probably because 'willn't' is quite difficult to say. Similarly, 'shall not' loses its 'll' as well as its 'o' and becomes 'shan't'.

In the second example above, although letters have been omitted from the first word as well as the second, only one apostrophe is used: it replaces the 'o' of 'not'. This is illogical but it looks better.

Revise

Have, Has and Had
- When 'have', 'has' or 'had' form part of the past tense of a verb, they are often contracted. Both the 'h' and the 'a' are omitted:
  - <u>They've</u> eaten all the cake.
  - <u>He's</u> been up all night.
  - <u>We'd</u> already read that chapter.
- Just as when 's indicates 'is', when 's is the shortened form of 'has' it can be used after a noun.
  - <u>Leila's</u> just come back from Lanzarote.
- 've is sometimes used after nouns but it looks and sounds clumsy:
  - <u>The cats've</u> gone into the garden.
- 'Has' and 'have' can also be shortened when they are used as main verbs, indicating belonging. This is more common in some places than others:
  - <u>We've</u> a blue car.

Modal Verbs
- When the **modal verb** 'would' is contracted, it loses all its letters except 'd':
  - <u>I'd</u> love to come but I'm much too busy.
  - <u>You'd</u> never believe who I've just seen.
- 'Would have', 'could have' and 'should have' can be shortened by omitting the 'ha' from 'have':
  - I <u>would've</u> loved that.
  - We <u>could've</u> got there on time if we'd rushed.

And
- 'And' is sometimes shortened to 'n', losing both 'a' and 'd':
  - fish <u>'n'</u> chips
  - rock <u>'n'</u> roll

Abbreviated Words
- Apostrophes can be used in words to indicate they have been shortened for informal use, particularly in dialogue:
  - because → 'cause
  - about → 'bout
- Some abbreviations have become so common that the apostrophe is no longer considered necessary:
  - telephone → phone
  - internet → net
- Words may be abbreviated in informal notes where the writer is sure that the meaning will be obvious to the reader:
  - government → gov't
  - appointment → app't

Quick Test
1. Why is an apostrophe no longer needed when abbreviating 'telephone'?
2. If two or more letters are omitted from a word, how many apostrophes are used?
3. Which two short words can 's replace?
4. What is the contracted form of 'would'?

Key Point
Omission (or contraction) is one of only two reasons for using the apostrophe. Letters omitted from words are replaced with apostrophes.

Key Point
The apostrophe for omission is used in informal speech and writing.

Key Words
contraction
dialogue
modal verb
omission
pronoun

The Apostrophe for Omission: Revise

The Apostrophe for Possession

You must be able to:
- Understand how apostrophes are used to show possession
- Use the apostrophe for possession accurately and confidently.

Possession

- Apostrophes (') can be used in two ways: to show **possession** and to indicate omission. Do not use them for any other reason.
- Possession means belonging. Use an apostrophe to show when something belongs to or is closely associated with someone or something.
- The apostrophe comes after the noun denoting the 'owner'.

Singular Nouns

- The usual way of showing possession is with an apostrophe followed by an 's':
  - The <u>dog's dinner</u>.
  - The <u>cat's whiskers</u>.

  It does not matter how many things are possessed. The dog has one dinner. The cat has several whiskers. However, there is only one dog and there is only one cat.

- This applies to all **singular** nouns, including those which end in 's':
  - <u>The lioness's cubs</u> are asleep.
  - <u>The class's behaviour</u> is appalling.

  It does not matter what letter a singular common nouns ends with. It is always followed by an apostrophe and 's' to show that something belongs to it.

- Many people have difficulty with proper nouns, particularly names, that end in 's'. The best thing to do is to treat them the same as any other singular noun: add an apostrophe and 's':
  - <u>Jess's homework</u> is excellent.
  - <u>Mr Jones's class</u> is on a trip.

- However, you will often see names that end in 's' followed just by an apostrophe:
  - <u>James' brother</u> was called Aaron.
  - <u>Ms Roberts' class</u> has stayed behind.

  Some authorities give 'rules' about this practice, but they differ. Some people say it is acceptable for long names but not short ones. Others say it should only be used for **classical** and **Biblical** names. There are others who think it is acceptable for any name ending in 's'. The good news is that, in the end, it is down to personal choice and you would not be penalised for doing it.

> **Key Point**
>
> Possession is one of only two reasons for using the apostrophe. The apostrophes show who owns what.

Revise

Plural Nouns

- When a **plural** noun ends in 's' (as most plural nouns do), simply add an apostrophe. There is no additional 's':
  - The bosses' meetings.
  - The girls' books.

  This second example demonstrates the importance of getting this right. If there were no apostrophe – the girls books – its meaning would be unclear. If the apostrophe is put before the 's' – the girl's books – we know that one girl has more than one book. With the apostrophe after 's' – the girls' books – we know that there is more than one book and these books belong to more than one girl.

- If one thing belongs to more than one person, you should still put an apostrophe after the final 's':
  - The girls' book.

  These unfortunate girls have to share a book.

- Names in the plural are treated the same way:
  - We're going to the Kellys' party.

- However, if the names of two people are joined, only the second one is given an apostrophe and, as it is a singular noun, it is followed by an apostrophe and 's'.
  - Ben and Jerry's ice cream is very popular.
  - I don't think I know Jill and Ross's parents.

- A plural noun that does not end in 's' is treated the same way as a singular noun. Just add an apostrophe and 's':
  - We enjoy children's games.
  - I've collected the geese's eggs.

Possessive Pronouns

- Possessive pronouns – because they already show possession – do not require apostrophes:
  - I liked the film but wasn't keen on its ending.
  - He put all his eggs in one basket. She put hers in two.
  - It isn't yours; it's ours.
  - The house is theirs now.

> **Key Point**
>
> You can show ownership by adding an apostrophe and 's' after a noun, unless it is a plural ending in 's'. In that case, just add an apostrophe.

> **Quick Test**
>
> 1. What should you add after a singular noun to show possession?
> 2. What should you add after a plural noun ending in 's' to show possession?
> 3. What should you use after a plural noun ending in any letter other than 's' to show possession?
> 4. Does the number of items possessed make any difference to your use of the apostrophe?
> 5. Are there any times when you should use the apostrophe apart from to show omission or possession?

> **Key Words**
>
> Biblical
> classical
> plural
> possession
> singular

The Apostrophe for Possession: Revise

Inverted Commas 1: Quotation and Titles

You must be able to:
- Use inverted commas for quotation and titles
- Understand when and how to use inverted commas in quotations.

Quotation

- Inverted commas ('...') are often referred to as '**speech marks**' or '**quotation marks**'. They are used for quotation and speech but neither of these terms covers all of their uses.
- When you quote, you are using somebody else's words. Quotation marks show the reader that this is the case:
  – According to Blenkinsop the situation is 'very serious'.
- There are different ways of setting out quotations.
- If the quotation consists of a single word or just a few words and fits naturally into your sentence without spoiling the sense, you simply put it in inverted commas:
  – In an attempt to persuade Romeo to stay, Juliet claims that 'It was the nightingale and not the lark' that they heard.
- If the quotation is fairly short (no more than forty words of **prose** or one line of **verse**) and you cannot fit it easily into your sentence, you can introduce it with a colon:
  – Juliet is adamant that it is not yet day: 'Believe me, love, it was the nightingale.'
- If you need to use a long quotation, still use a colon but start a new line and **indent**. You must indent the whole quotation and, if quoting verse, end the lines where they end in the original text. In this case you do not use inverted commas:
  – Juliet is anxious that Romeo should not leave and tries to persuade him that it is not yet day:
      It was the nightingale and not the lark
      That pierced the fearful hollow of thine ear.
- It is essential that any text you put within quotation marks is exactly the same as in the original. It must be spelt and punctuated as in the original, even if you think the original spelling and punctuation are incorrect.
- The use of quotation marks around a word or phrase can imply the writer considers the word or phrase to be inaccurate, misleading, or not being used in the normal or standard sense:
  – He may well be a 'man of the people', but which people?
In these cases, the words in the inverted commas may or may not be direct quotations. By using quotation marks, the writer is making it clear that he / she would not normally use those words in that context.

> Using quotations in this way is known as '**embedding**' and it is encouraged by teachers and examiners, so it should be the method you use most often.

> **Key Point**
>
> Inverted commas are often referred to as quotation marks because they are used to show that the words within them are not the writer's own words.

Revise

- Closing inverted commas come after any punctuation which is part of the quotation:
  - Juliet says that the nightingale 'pierced the fearful hollow of thine ear.'
  Here the full stop is in the original text.
- Punctuation might need to be added after the closing inverted comma:
  - Juliet insists that Romeo heard 'the nightingale and not the lark'.

> Here a full stop is needed to end the sentence but, as the quotation does not end with one, it must be added after the closing inverted comma.

Titles

- Inverted commas are used around titles of poems, articles, books, films etc.:
  - We've been studying 'The Eagle' by Tennyson.
- In print or type-written work, the usual practice is to put the titles of longer works, such as films or novels, in italics, dispensing with the inverted commas:
  - I prefer *Great Expectations* to *Pride and Prejudice*.
- However, the usual convention is still to put titles of poems, short stories and articles in inverted commas:
  - Shelby's article 'Farming in the Early Sixteenth Century' was published in *Agriculture through the Ages*, edited by McLean.
- These are not hard and fast rules, however, and in handwritten work you should use inverted commas around all titles.
- Most words in titles should be capitalised, including the first and last words. Other short conjunctions, prepositions and articles are not capitalised:
  - 'The War of the Worlds'
- There is a growing trend, especially in newspapers, to write titles without using inverted commas or italics, instead relying on capital letters to show the phrase is a title. This can be confusing at times, so it is best not to do it in your own work.

Double Inverted Commas

- Double inverted commas ("…") should be used when the words being quoted include a quotation, speech or title:
  - Cory criticises the 'sort of people who use words like "literally" when they mean the exact opposite.'

> **Key Point**
>
> Everything inside the quotation marks should be written exactly as in the original text, even if the spelling and punctuation is incorrect.

Quick Test

1. When should you embed a quotation?
2. What punctuation mark is used to introduce a quotation that is not embedded?
3. Would you use inverted commas if you were quoting four lines of poetry?
4. When should you use double inverted commas?

Key Words

embed
indent
prose
quotation marks
speech marks
verse

Inverted Commas 1: Quotation and Titles: Revise

Inverted Commas 2: Punctuating Speech

You must be able to:
- Use inverted commas for direct speech
- Punctuate direct speech correctly.

Speech Marks

- Inverted commas ('…') are often referred to as 'speech marks' because they are used to show direct speech.
- Direct speech is the actual words spoken by a person:
  She said, 'I think we should club together for a present'.
- **Indirect** or **reported speech** may paraphrase the speaker's words and does not require inverted commas:
  - She suggested that we should club together for a present.
  - She said we should share the cost of the present.

Punctuation of Direct Speech

- A comma is used to introduce speech and is outside the inverted commas:
  - He asked, 'Who is that masked man?'
- However, when the 'said' element comes after the speech or in the middle of the speech, a comma is placed before the closing inverted comma:
  - 'I haven't got a clue,' she replied.
  - 'Somebody,' he said, 'must know.'
- A full stop may be used after the main verb ('said' etc.) and before the inverted comma, marking the resumption of speech and showing that the speaker has finished one sentence and is starting another.
  - 'Somebody must know,' she agreed. 'I wish I did.'
- As in the example above, when the speech or part of it comes after the 'said' element, punctuation to end the speech goes within the speech marks:
  - He asked, 'Are we there yet?'

New Speaker, New Line

- The 'new speaker, new line' rule might be more accurately expressed as 'new speaker, new paragraph'.
- If you are writing a conversation using direct speech, it is important to know when a new person is speaking. Starting a new line prevents **ambiguity**.
- When you start the new line, do it in the same way as starting a new paragraph, indenting or leaving a line:
  - Joey said, 'I'll meet you at the station.'
    'That's okay,' Sara replied. 'I can get a taxi.'

> **Key Point**
>
> As with quotations, you should always put all the spoken words within the speech marks.

Revise

- You do not need to start a new paragraph if nobody has previously spoken in the current one:
  - Joey knew Sara would be arriving soon and he was worried about her getting home. He decided to phone her. She answered. Joey said, 'I'll meet you at the station.'
- Similarly, you can continue your paragraph after the direct speech until somebody new speaks:
  - 'That's okay,' Sara replied. 'I can get a taxi.' She finished the call without saying goodbye and picked up her bags.
- 'New speaker, new line' is especially important if you stop using 'she said' etc.:
  - 'Where are you?'
    'I don't know.'
    'Haven't you got a map?'

Take care when doing this. If the conversation goes on too long without the names of the speakers, it can become confusing.

Double Inverted Commas

- You will see double inverted commas ("…") used for direct speech in a lot of publications, especially older editions and books that use American English.
- It is preferable to use single inverted commas, however, to avoid confusion if you need to use inverted commas within speech:
  - Joey said, 'She said "I'll get a taxi" but I don't think she can afford it.'
  - 'I wrote about "My Last Duchess" and "Jabberwocky" in the exam.'

When not to use Inverted Commas for Speech

- In some books you might see dashes used instead of inverted commas to mark direct speech. It is better not to do this in your own work.
- Do not use inverted commas in indirect speech:
  - She asked where she could find a taxi.
  - He said that he had not realised what was going on.
- Do not use inverted commas when writing dialogue in a script:
  - Sara: Where are you?
    Joey: I don't know.
    Sara: Haven't you got a map?

> ### Quick Test
> 1. Which of these requires the use of inverted commas – direct or indirect speech?
> 2. Which punctuation mark is used to introduce direct speech?
> 3. How do you show that a new person is speaking?
> 4. What is the alternative, in print, to using inverted commas for titles?
> 5. Should you use speech marks for dialogue in a play script?

> **Key Point**
>
> Inverted commas are often referred to as speech marks because they are used to start and finish direct speech.

> **Key Point**
>
> Try not to overuse direct speech. It is useful in **narrative** writing but sometimes indirect speech can be more effective.

> **Key Words**
>
> ambiguity
> indirect speech
> narrative
> reported speech

Inverted Commas 2: Punctuating Speech: Revise

Practice Questions

The Apostrophe

1 Rewrite the following sentences using the apostrophe to show omission.

   a) I will not go. _____

   b) We can not do it. _____

   c) That is not yours. _____

   d) They are over there. _____

   e) She is in the other room. _____

   f) I shall not be there. _____ [6]

2 Rewrite the following phrases using an apostrophe to show possession.

   a) The uncle of my mother _____

   b) The hamsters of Jonny _____

   c) The office of the boss _____

   d) The friends of Anna and Samina _____

   e) The room of the women _____ [5]

3 The following passage has been written without apostrophes. Insert apostrophes as appropriate. There should be **ten**.

My sisters friend from France is coming to stay with us for a week. Shes going to have my brother Toms room because hes away at university. It took us days to tidy all his things. Luckily she isnt a fussy eater, according to Lia. I hope she likes pizzas because thats about all Lia will eat. Mum thinks shell probably need a healthier diet, however, so she went to the greengrocers today and came back with potatoes, tomatoes, courgettes and some weird looking things Id never seen before. Lia says I mustnt try to speak to her in French but Mrs Jones says I need the practice. [10]

Practise

Inverted Commas

4 Below is a short stanza of poetry.

> The night was dark, no father was there.
> The child was wet with dew;
> The mire was deep, and the child did weep,
> And away the vapour flew.
>
> William Blake, 'The Little Boy Lost'

Insert inverted commas (quotation marks) in the correct place in each sentence.

a) Blake uses words such as night and dark to create a sense of danger.

b) The picture of the child, wet with dew, invokes sympathy.

c) Suddenly the danger is gone: And away the vapour flew.

d) The Little Boy Lost is a very disturbing poem. [4]

5 Insert speech marks correctly in the sentences that follow:

a) He said, Let's go to the cinema.

b) Would you like a slice of cake? Mary asked.

c) I would like one, he replied, but I'd better not. [3]

6 Tick the **five** sentences in which inverted commas are used correctly.

a) According to her, the experience was 'heartbreakingly hilarious'. ☐

b) I'm reading 'Hard Times by Charles Dickens'. ☐

c) I've just finished 'Hard Times' by Charles Dickens. ☐

d) 'That's marvellous!' she exclaimed. ☐

e) Lady Macbeth thinks 'a little water' will wash away her guilt. ☐

f) I told her that 'I only had a little water.' ☐

g) 'If I were you she said I would try the chocolate flavour.' ☐

h) He paused before saying, 'I prefer coffee.' ☐ [5]

Review Questions

Ending Sentences, and Commas

1 The following passage has been punctuated using only commas. **Five** of these have been used incorrectly instead of full stops. Underline them.

Knowing that we were about to run out of tea and biscuits, I went to the corner shop, it was shut, I had to change my plans and go to the supermarket, which is twenty minutes' walk away, however, I had plenty of time and, besides, I enjoy walking, unfortunately, by the time I got there I had completely forgotten what I had gone for, [5]

2 Insert **two** commas correctly in each of these sentences:

a) I bought coffee bread milk and apples.

b) As I was approaching the checkout I bumped into Mo who lives across the road.

c) Mo said 'You haven't got much shopping have you?'

d) 'I only wanted tea' I replied 'and a packet of garibaldis.'

e) Mo a person who thinks life is one big joke collapsed into helpless laughter. [10]

3 Tick the **five** sentences or groups of sentences below that have been correctly punctuated.

a) I spoke to Mr Austin. Who was walking his dogs. ☐

b) After I left Mr Austin, I started walking more quickly. ☐

c) A squirrel shot out, from the bushes. ☐

d) You see quite a lot of wildlife round here: squirrels, hedgehogs, foxes and all sorts of birds. ☐

e) Someone asked me if I knew the way to the post office? ☐

f) 'There isn't one for miles', I replied, 'You might need to get a bus.' ☐

g) I showed her the way to the bus stop! ☐

h) I waited with her until the bus came. ☐

i) Did I enjoy the day? Yes, I suppose I did. ☐

j) I had tea, then I went for a walk. ☐ [5]

Review

Colons, Semicolons, Hyphens and Slashes, and Parethesis and Ellipsis

4 Which punctuation mark should you use for the following purposes? Choose from:

　　　colon　　semicolon　　ellipsis　　hyphen　　slash

　a) to separate items in a list

　b) to introduce a list

　c) to give alternative words

　d) to form a compound word

　e) to introduce a quotation

　f) to link two closely related clauses

　g) to show that some words have been omitted

　h) to introduce an explanation after a statement

　i) to create suspense at the end of a sentence

　j) to show where a line of poetry ends in a short quotation　　[10]

5 Insert a hyphen or hyphens, or forward slash in the correct places in the following sentences.

　a) Omniscient means the same as all knowing.

　b) I am happy to look after any dog cat for a fair price.

　c) We're having tea with Julia Carrington Brown.

　d) I'll take the blue one and or the red one.

　e) He'll be eighty nine tomorrow.　　[5]

6 The following sentences all contain dashes. What other punctuation mark could be used to replace the dashes?

　a) I like apples – she prefers pears.

　b) Nobody – I mean absolutely nobody – believes that story.

　c) We won the prize – our project was the most successful.

　d) And the winner is – Elliot!

　e) Abraham – tall, thin, about thirty – works at the garage.　　[5]

Grammar

Nouns

You must be able to:
- Understand what a noun is and understand what is meant by common or concrete, proper, abstract, and collective nouns
- Use all types of nouns appropriately in your writing.

Parts of Speech

- The phrase 'parts of speech' refers to the way in which words are used.
- The phrase 'word class' is often used to mean the same thing.
- Traditionally the eight parts of speech in English are: **nouns**, pronouns, adjectives, **verbs**, adverbs, **prepositions**, **conjunctions** and **interjections**. Many people add a ninth class: **determiners**.
- It is important to remember that the same word can be a different part of speech, depending on its function.
  - In 'I love ice cream', 'love' is a verb.
  - In 'Love conquers all', 'love' is a noun.
- Nouns are naming words.
- There are four kinds of noun: proper nouns, common nouns (also called **concrete nouns**), abstract nouns, and collective nouns.

Proper Nouns

- Proper nouns name people, places, days of the week and months of the year.
- A proper noun is specific, not general:
  - Greece: there is only one country called Greece.
  - James: there are a lot of people called James but the proper noun identifies him because it belongs to him. It is used instead of 'the boy' or 'him', for example.
  - Thursday: there is a new Thursday every week but using the proper noun pinpoints the day within the week: 'next Thursday' rather than 'in the next few days'.
- Proper nouns always start with capital letters. Other nouns (like all other words) start with a capital letter only when they start a new sentence.
- Adjectives or other nouns can form part of a proper noun and when they do they start with capitals:
  - Black Wednesday
  - Bollington High School

  'Bollington High School' is a **compound noun**, as it is made up of more than one noun but names a single thing.
- Words that are normally common nouns can become proper nouns because of the way in which they are used:
  - We have studied all the <u>kings and queens</u> of England.

> **Key Point**
>
> Proper nouns, such as the names of people and places, start with a capital letter.

> **Key Point**
>
> In older texts you might see nouns that are not proper nouns starting with capitals. Often there is no logical explanation for this except that the writer thought the words were important. It is not acceptable practice now.

Here 'queen' is a common noun.
- The Queen is coming to open the library.

Here 'The Queen' counts as being her name. The same applies to names of family members, so 'Mum' and 'Dad' are proper nouns but 'my mum' and 'your dad' are not.

Common Nouns and Abstract Nouns

- A **common noun**, also known as a concrete noun, is the name of something physical that you can touch or feel (in the literal sense), hear, taste or see.
  - Table – you can see and touch the table.
  - Wind – you can hear it and you can feel it.
- **Abstract nouns** are the names of ideas, emotions, concepts or feelings (not in the literal sense):
  - It was a case of true love.
  - It will take hours to get there.
  - I'm having trouble with the arithmetic.
- The same noun can be a common or an abstract noun, often because the noun is being used metaphorically:
  - The Earth's atmosphere is changing.
  - There was a great atmosphere at the game.

Collective Nouns

- A **collective noun** is a noun that treats a group of people or things as one entity:
  - A class is made up of individual pupils.
  - A herd is a group of cows.
- Collective nouns are singular. When a collective noun is the subject of a sentence the verb is formed as if it were a single person or thing:
  - Our team is top of the league.
  - The Government issued a statement yesterday.
- A proper noun, for example the name of a team or company, can be a collective noun:
  - Arsenal has had a bad start this season.

Noun Phrases

- A **noun phrase** is a term for a group of words, including a noun, that acts as the noun in a clause, whether as the subject or the object of the noun.
- A noun phrase tells you more about the noun and can include any other part of speech:
  - That house is beautiful.
  - I like the house with the bay windows.
  - My uncle's house is on the road to Birkenhead.

> **Quick Test**
>
> 1. What is the term for nouns that name individual people?
> 2. Is a word that names an idea a common or an abstract noun?
> 3. Are collective nouns singular or plural?

Revise

Key Point

Common or concrete nouns name things that are tangible; abstract nouns name ideas, feelings and concepts.

'Atmosphere' here is a common noun because, although you cannot actually touch it, the atmosphere is a physical thing.

'Atmosphere' here refers to an idea or perception so it is an abstract noun.

Key Point

In speech and informal writing many people treat collective nouns as if they were plurals. However, in formal writing you should always treat them as singular.

Key Words

abstract noun
collective noun
common noun
compound noun
concrete noun
conjunction
determiner
interjection
noun
noun phrase
preposition
verb

Nouns: Revise   53

Pronouns

You must be able to:
- Understand what is meant by pronouns, including relative and possessive pronouns
- Use all types of pronoun appropriately in your writing.

Personal Pronouns

- Pronouns replace nouns and perform the same function in grammar.
- Using pronouns means you can avoid constantly repeating the same noun, which can be time-consuming and irritating.
- Which pronoun you use depends on four things: number (singular or plural), person (first, second or third); **gender** (male, female or **neuter**) and case (subject or **object**).
- This table shows all the English **personal pronouns**.

> **Key Point**
>
> Pronouns replace nouns to avoid repetition.

	Person	Singular male	Singular female	Singular neuter	Plural (all genders)
Subject	First person	I	I	I	we
	Second person	you	you	you	you
	Third person	he	she	it	they
Object	First person	me	me	me	us
	Second person	you	you	you	you
	Third person	him	her	it	them

- The most common misuse of personal pronouns is the confusion of 'I' and 'me'. 'I' is the subject of the clause'; 'me' is the object.
- 'Me and Annie are going out' is wrong because you and Annie are the subjects of the sentence. You would not say: 'Me is going out.' You should say: '<u>Annie and I</u> are going out'.
- In the same way, you should not say 'They praised Art and I' because you would not say, 'They praised I'. The correct form is: 'They praised <u>Art and me</u>.'
- To refer to a person as either male or female, many writers use 'he / she', 's/he' or 'they'.
- Variations on 'she / he' do not present grammatical problems and their meaning, therefore, is clearer.
- In many cases the 'gender neutral' conundrum can be avoided by using plural forms correctly:
  - If <u>readers</u> wish, <u>they</u> can borrow up to six books.

> **Key Point**
>
> In English, male and female pronouns usually only apply to people and animals. You will sometimes see a ship or car referred to as 'she', however.

> **Key Point**
>
> 'Anyone', 'anything', 'everyone' and 'everything' are also pronouns.

Relative Pronouns

- **Relative pronouns** relate (or refer) to someone or something that has already been mentioned and usually link a subordinate clause to the main clause of a sentence.
- The relative pronouns are 'who', 'whom', 'which', 'that' and 'whose' (the possessive relative). They can be singular or plural.
- 'Who' and 'whom' refer to people. 'Who' is used when the person or persons are the subject of the clause and 'whom' when they are the object:
    - Maria is the woman <u>who</u> sang at the concert.
    - Maria, <u>whom</u> I met yesterday, sang in the concert.
- 'Which' refers to things, whether they are the subject or object:
    - The chair, <u>which</u> was in the garage, was broken.
- 'That' can replace 'which'. It is less formal:
    - The chair <u>that</u> was in the garage is broken.

Possessive Pronouns

- **Possessive pronouns** are used to indicate possession without repeating nouns.
- The strong possessive pronouns are 'mine', 'yours', 'hers', 'his', 'its', 'ours', 'yours' and 'theirs'. They refer back to a noun and replace it to avoid repetition. They come after a verb:
    - That coat is <u>mine</u>. (rather than 'that coat is my coat')
- The weak possessive pronouns are 'my', 'your', 'her', 'his', 'its', 'our', 'your' and 'their'. They are used before nouns and can also be classed as adjectives or determiners (see pages 56–57):
    - Give me <u>your</u> hat.
- 'Whose' is the possessive form of who, whom and which:
    - <u>Whose</u> rabbit is that?
    - The rabbit, <u>whose</u> ears are brown, belongs to Jack.

Emphatic / Reflexive Pronouns

- 'Myself', 'yourself', 'herself', 'himself', 'ourselves', yourselves' and 'themselves' are used in two ways: as **emphatic pronouns** or **reflexive pronouns**.
- You can use them to give added force to a statement (emphatic):
    - <u>I</u> did the whole thing <u>myself</u>.
- You can use them when the same person or thing is the object and subject (reflexive):
    - <u>The dog</u> has only <u>himself</u> to blame.
- They must **not** be used instead of personal pronouns, for example: 'myself and Jim will be in charge' or 'she did it to myself.'

> **Quick Test**
>
> 1. Which four factors influence which personal pronoun is used?
> 2. What is the plural of 'you'?
> 3. Which two relative pronouns can be either weak or strong?

Revise

Key Point

Relative pronouns connect subordinate clauses with main causes.

'Whom' is rarely used in speech or informal writing, 'who' being used instead.

Key Words

emphatic pronoun
gender
neuter
object
personal pronoun
possessive pronoun
reflexive pronoun
relative pronoun

Grammar

Adjectives and Determiners

You must be able to:

- Understand what adjectives and determiners are
- Use adjectives and determiners effectively to improve your writing.

Types of Adjectives

- Adjectives are often referred to as 'describing words' because they describe nouns.
- Not all adjectives give a description, however, so it is more accurate to say that they **modify** nouns or limit them. As part of a noun phrase, an adjective gives information about the noun.
- Adjectives that come before the noun are known as prepositional adjectives:
  - The blue door.
  - My brilliant idea.
- Adjectives which are placed after the noun are postpositional adjectives:
  - The door is blue.
  - My idea was brilliant.
- Normalised adjectives are adjectives which function as nouns. This means that an adjective is used without a noun:
  - His is the red door; mine is the blue.
  - The great and the good.
- A lot of adjectives end in 'ed' or 'ing'. These are known as **participle adjectives** because they are **participles** of verbs, which are also used to form the tenses of verbs:
  - The frightened rabbit.

  This means the same as 'the rabbit which is / was frightened' but instead of being part of a passive verb, 'frightened' has become an adjective.
  - The shining sun.

  This is a quicker and neater way of saying 'the sun which is shining' or 'the sun which was shining'. The participle (part of the verb) has become an adjective.

Here the word 'blue' is used on its own instead of 'the blue door' or 'the blue one'. The noun is assumed.

Here both adjectives are used without nouns. It is clear to the reader that the writer is referring to great people and good people.

Use of Adjectives

- Adjectives can be used to identify something or somebody:
  - It's in the red file.
  - The file you want is red.

  The adjective is used so that we know which file is being referred to.
- Adjectives are used to give extra information. This could be factual information to tell the reader more about something or somebody:
  - I approached the red door nervously.

  Here the adjective is not essential, as it was in the case of the red file.

Key Point

Adjectives modify or limit nouns by giving more information.

Examiners like to see adjectives but try not to overuse them. Only use them in non-fiction writing when they are necessary.

56   KS3 Spelling, Punctuation and Grammar Revision Guide

Revise

- The information might be subjective, telling us about the writer as well as the person or thing being described:
  - My idea was <u>brilliant</u>.

  This is what the writer thinks of the idea. Others might disagree.
- Adjectives are very useful in creative writing. By describing people, places and feelings you can give a more complete picture to the reader and create an appropriate atmosphere:
  - A <u>curious black</u> cow edged towards us.
- Remember that in descriptive writing you can use adjectives to show not only what is seen, but also what is heard, felt, smelled or tasted. Use all five senses:
  - A <u>screeching</u> bell interrupted us.
  - The air was <u>damp</u> and <u>clammy</u>.

Determiners

- **Determiners** are short words that come before nouns or at the beginning of noun phrases and indicate what they refer to.
- In traditional grammar, determiners are usually classed as adjectives.
- Determiners include articles (definite and indefinite), possessive determiners, demonstratives, **quantifiers** and numbers.
- The **definite article** is 'the'. Its use means that you are referring to a particular thing or things:
  - <u>The</u> cat is hungry.

  The cat is a particular cat whose identity both speaker and listener are aware of. 'The' is used with both singular and plural nouns.
- The **indefinite article** is 'a' (or 'an' before a vowel):
  - There is <u>a</u> cat in the garden.

  We do not know this cat.
- Plural nouns do not require indefinite articles:
  - There are <u>cats</u> in the garden.
- Traditionally, possessive pronouns such as 'my' and 'your' that come before the noun have been described as adjectives. Now they are often called possessive determiners.
- Like possessive determiners, demonstrative determiners (that, this, those) narrow down what is being referred to:
  - I want <u>that</u> one.
- Quantifiers (some, few, more etc.) tell us how much of something there is, while numbers tell us how many:
  - I'd like <u>some</u> cake.   – I've eaten <u>three</u> cakes.

Quick Test

1. What sort of word does an adjective modify?
2. From what class of word is a participle adjective formed?
3. What is the definite article?
4. Give an alternative term for a possessive determiner.

> **Key Point**
>
> Determiners, including the definite article, perform a similar function to adjectives.

> **Key Words**
>
> definite article
> indefinite article
> modify
> participle
> participle adjective
> quantifier

Adjectives and Determiners: Revise

Conjunctions

You must be able to:
- Understand how to use coordinating and subordinating conjunctions
- Use conjunctions effectively to improve your writing.

Conjunctions

- Conjunctions are words or short phrases that are used to link words, phrases, clauses and sentences.
- A conjunction is a type of **connective** but not all connectives are conjunctions. Connectives can also be adverbs, adverbial phrases, and relative pronouns. Try not to confuse the two words.
- Different conjunctions have different functions.

Coordinating Conjunctions

- 'And', 'but' and 'or' are one-word **coordinating conjunctions**. By 'coordinating' the words, phrases or clauses, the conjunctions give them equal status.
- The words themselves signal different relationships between the things being coordinated.
- 'And' and 'or' can be used to link single words or even prefixes:
  - Sam is a black <u>and</u> white cat.
  - You can choose chips <u>or</u> mash.
  - I'll discuss pro- <u>and</u> anti-establishment views.
- 'And', 'but' and 'or' can link phrases:
  - It was very beautiful <u>but</u> extremely expensive.
- When coordinating conjunctions are used to link two clauses, they create a compound sentence (see page 77):
  - Jed wanted to speak to Lou <u>but</u> he had lost his phone.
- Coordinating conjunctions can consist of two words: ('both… and'; 'either…or'; 'neither…nor'):
  - They wanted <u>neither</u> chips <u>nor</u> mash.
  - <u>Both</u> the lasagne <u>and</u> the ratatouille are delicious.

Subordinating Conjunctions

- **Subordinating conjunctions** link words, phrases or clauses to show that they are not of equal importance. They are most commonly used to link clauses.
- When a subordinating conjunction links two clauses, they become a complex sentence (see pages 78–79). The subordinating conjunction comes at the beginning of the subordinate clause to show that it is of less importance than the main clause.

> **Key Point**
>
> You should not normally use conjunctions to start sentences. However, they are used occasionally for impact. If used too frequently they lose their impact.
>
> We arrived at eight-thirty. <u>But</u> we left immediately.

> **Key Point**
>
> Conjunctions are words that are used to link words, phrases or clauses.

Revise

- Subordinating conjunctions can consist of more than one word.
- Different subordinating conjunctions show different relationships between the words, phrases or clauses linked.
- They can refer to time:
  - I'll see Caroline <u>before</u> Andrew.
  - <u>When</u> I've finished the washing, I'll do the ironing.
  - I will give it in <u>as soon as</u> it's finished.
- They can refer to place:
  - She told me <u>where</u> she had left it.
  - I will keep trying <u>until</u> I get it right.
- They can show cause and effect, giving the reasons for what is happening in the main clause:
  - I climbed the mountain <u>because</u> it was there.
  - <u>As</u> I want to get good marks, I intend to study tonight.
- They can indicate the **condition** under which things happen in the main clause:
  - <u>If</u> you want to get to Scunthorpe, you should take the train.
  - I won't go <u>unless</u> you go with me.
- Conjunctions of **concession** show the context of an action that takes place in spite of something that could have prevented it:
  - <u>Although</u> he can be difficult, I think he shows promise.
  - I'm going ahead with the race <u>despite</u> the gloomy weather forecasts.
- Conjunctions can introduce a comparison:
  - Michael takes the bus, <u>whereas</u> Jody travels by train.
  - <u>In contrast to</u> the bustle of the city, Middlington is quiet and peaceful.

> **Key Point**
>
> Coordinating conjunctions link clauses of equal value; subordinating conjunctions show the relationship between clauses of unequal importance.

Examples of Subordinating Conjunctions

Time	Place	Cause	Condition	Concession	Comparison
after	where	as	if	although	in contrast to
as	wherever	because	in case	despite	whereas
as soon as		in order to	provided that	in spite of	while*
before		since	unless	though	
when		so			
whenever		so that			
while					

* Depending on the context, conjunctions of comparison can also be seen as coordinating conjunctions.

> **Quick Test**
>
> 1. Are connectives always conjunctions?
> 2. Are conjunctions always connectives?
> 3. What sort of conjunction is 'but'?
> 4. What sort of clause does a subordinating conjunction start?
> 5. Of what sort of subordinating conjunction are 'if' and 'unless' examples?

> **Key Words**
>
> concession
> condition
> connective
> coordinating conjunction
> subordinating conjunction

Practice Questions

Nouns

1 Identify the nouns in the following sentences.

　a) The wall is too high to climb.

　b) All children love toffee.

　c) It is important to obey the law at all times.

　d) My brother's going to Scarborough on a train.

　e) Hindsight is a wonderful thing. [10]

2 What sort of noun are the following words? Choose from:

　　　　abstract　　　collective　　　common　　　proper

　Some of the words may belong to more than one group.

　a) Amanda

　b) banjo

　c) delight

　d) elephant

　e) Friday

　f) gallantry

　g) herd

　h) juice [8]

Pronouns

3 In the following sentences replace the nouns in bold with appropriate pronouns.

　a) **The girl** won the race.

　b) **Jo and Jack** are friends.

　c) I saw **Jo and Jack** yesterday.

Practise

    d) I will see **the girl** today.

    e) **The girl** did not see **the boy**. [6]

Adjectives and Determiners

4 Identify the adjectives in the following sentences.

    a) It was a lovely day today.

    b) There might be light showers tomorrow, apparently.

    c) I'll have to get a new umbrella.

    d) You can share mine. It's huge.

    e) I'm very grateful but I wanted one anyway. [5]

5 Which of the following pairs of sentences is correct? Underline the answers.

    a) Me and Rollo are brothers. / Rollo and I are brothers.

    b) Them are great chips. / They are great chips.

    c) They sent a present to Jan and me. / They sent a present to Jan and I.

    d) They is a good person. / They are good people.

    e) Us aren't happy today. / We aren't happy today. [5]

Conjunctions

6 Insert an appropriate conjunction in each of the following sentences. Choose from:

    although   and   because   but   if

    a) I like apples _____ pears.

    b) _____ you come round later, I'll lend you that book.

    c) I had to leave early _____ I was feeling sick.

    d) _____ I'd met her several times, I didn't recognise her today.

    e) I ate the apple _____ I couldn't manage the pear. [5]

Review Questions

Apostrophes

1 Insert apostrophes in the following sentences where appropriate.

a) I know its not the best work weve ever done.

b) Ladies clothing is on the first floor and gentlemens on the third.

c) Thats not yours; its ours.

d) Ill give you my classs marks as soon as Ive finished them.

e) The whole familys coming for tea. [10]

2 Each of the following sentences contains a mistake. On a separate piece of paper, rewrite each sentence correctly.

a) Give me you're pencil.

b) We played domino's.

c) It's all your's.

d) There were two failures and eight pass's.

e) I lost my key's.

f) Dan's and Dora's mother's called Doris.

g) He's left his' wallet behind.

h) I wont be trying that again.

i) I don't know we're I left it.

j) Joanna's selling piano's. [10]

3 Which **four** of the following statements about apostrophes are true?

a) You should always use an apostrophe before the letter 's'. ☐

b) Apostrophes are used to show belonging. ☐

c) Apostrophes should be placed after 's' in plurals that end in 's'. ☐

d) Apostrophes can be used for emphasis. ☐

e) Apostrophes are used to show omission. ☐

f) Every letter omitted should be replaced with an apostrophe. ☐

g) To show possession a plural not ending in 's' is followed by an apostrophe and an 's'. ☐ [4]

Review

Inverted Commas

4 Tick the **five** sentences below that have been correctly punctuated.

a) 'I don't know about you,' she said, 'but I'm exhausted.' ☐

b) 'Jimmy' got a prize for his project. ☐

c) The project was about 'polar bears and penguins'. ☐

d) Jimmy's project was called 'Polar Bears and Penguins'. ☐

e) Juliet compares Romeo to a flower: 'A rose by any other name would smell as sweet.' ☐

f) She calls it a 'rose garden' but there are no roses. ☐

g) 'Would you like some help?' she asked. ☐ [5]

5 Insert inverted commas correctly in each of these sentences:

a) I've just finished reading The Lion the Witch and the Wardrobe.

b) I asked, Would you like to borrow it?

c) They are referred to as star cross'd lovers.

d) She's having what she always calls forty winks.

e) It would be much better, he said, to get a good night's sleep. [5]

6 Which **four** of the following statements about inverted commas are true?

a) Inverted commas are often referred to as 'speech marks'. ☐

b) Inverted commas are used around titles. ☐

c) You always use inverted commas when referring to a text, even if paraphrasing. ☐

d) You can use inverted commas to show something is important. ☐

e) When quoting you should retain the original spelling and punctuation. ☐

f) In direct speech the inverted commas include all the words spoken. ☐ [4]

Verbs 1: Tenses

You must be able to:
- Understand what tenses do and how they are formed
- Use a range of correctly formed tenses in your writing.

Tenses

- Verbs are often referred to as 'doing words'. In fact, they express both action (doing and thinking) and states (being and feeling).
- Each verb has an **infinitive**, which is the basic form of the verb:
  - I would like <u>to see</u> it.
- Verbs have different tenses that tell us whether something has happened (past), is happening (present) or will happen (future).

Present Tense

- There are two forms: **simple present** and present continuous.
- The simple present shows that something is happening now that is not expected to stop, or is habitual or repeated:
  - I <u>love</u> badminton.   – I <u>go</u> to badminton every week.
- The present continuous shows that an ongoing action is happening at the moment of speech. It is formed by using the verb 'to be' and a present participle (ending in 'ing'):
  - I <u>am eating</u> my dinner.
- It can also be used informally as a future tense:
  - I <u>am playing</u> badminton tonight.
- Most verbs follow this pattern:

	Singular	Plural
Simple present	I / you / she / he sleeps.	We / you / they sleep.
Present continuous	I am sleeping. You are sleeping. He / she / it is sleeping.	We / you / they are sleeping.

Future Tense

- There are four future tenses.
- The **simple future** is used for an action that will happen in the future.
  - I <u>shall go</u> to the market tomorrow.
- The **future continuous** is used for an ongoing action that will happen in the future.
  - They <u>will be travelling</u> tonight.
- The **future perfect** is used for an action that will have been completed at some point in the future.
  - By the end of the year <u>he will have completed</u> six marathons.

> **Key Point**
>
> Each tense has several different forms, giving different meanings. It is important that you use the right tense to convey your meaning and that there is agreement between your subject and verb.

> **Key Point**
>
> Present participles of all verbs are formed by adding 'ing' to the infinitive but past participles can vary.

> **Key Point**
>
> There are three basic tenses: past, present and future.

Revise

- The **future perfect continuous** is used for an ongoing action that will have been completed at a point in the future.
  - When they get there they <u>will have been travelling</u> for hours.

Past Tense

- There are four past tenses. Most errors in tenses are caused by confusion of the various forms of the past tense.
- Another common error is the confusion of the **simple past** tense and the **perfect tense** in irregular verbs, for example 'we done' instead of 'we did'.
- The simple past is used to show something has finished. It is usually formed by adding 'ed' to the infinitive but there are many exceptions:
  - We <u>bowled</u> first.   – They <u>made</u> it last week.
- The **past continuous** is used for an action that was ongoing in the past.
  - They <u>were painting</u> the wall when the post came.
- The perfect tense is used to show an action has been completed.
  - We <u>have</u> already <u>seen</u> it.
- The **past perfect** is used for actions further back in the past when the past tense has already been used.
  - We told her <u>we had painted</u> the wall.
- Most verbs (referred to as regular verbs) follow this pattern, see below:

	Singular	Plural
Simple past	I / he / she / it walked.	We / you / they walked.
Past continuous	I was walking. He / she / it was walking. They were walking.	We / you / they were walking.
Perfect	I have walked. You have walked. He / she / it has walked.	We you / they have walked.
Past perfect	I / you / he / she / it had walked.	We / you / they had walked.

- There are many irregular verbs. In order to form their past tenses correctly you need to know their simple past forms as well as their present and past participles.

Infinitive	Simple past	Past participle
be	I was, you were, he / she / it was, we / you / they were	been
eat	ate	eaten
do	did	done
give	gave	given
get	got	got
lie	lay	laid
sing	sang	sung
ring	rang	rung
see	saw	seen
speak	spoke	spoken
teach	taught	taught
go	went	gone
wake	woke	woken
beat	beat	beaten
take	took	taken
rise	rose	risen
break	broke	broken

Key Point

Different forms of past, present and future tenses are used to convey different meanings.

Key Words

future continuous
future perfect
future perfect continuous
infinitive
past continuous
past perfect
perfect tense
simple future
simple past
simple present

Quick Test

1. What are the two forms of the present tense called?
2. Which verb is used with the present participle to form the present continuous tense?
3. How do present participles end?
4. How is the perfect tense formed?

Verbs 1: Tenses: Revise

Verbs 2

You must be able to:
- Use active and passive voices accurately and effectively
- Use a range of modal verbs accurately and effectively.

Transitive and Intransitive Verbs

- Verbs can be either **transitive** or **intransitive**. A transitive verb must have a direct object:
  - I told her what had happened.
  'Her' is the object of the action, so 'told' is a transitive verb.
  - Magpies steal jewellery.
  'Steal' is a transitive verb and 'jewellery' is its object.
- A verb without a direct object cannot be transitive:
  - They are running.
  'Are running' is an intransitive verb.
- An intransitive verb can have an indirect object. Its relationship to the object is shown by a preposition (see pages 70–71):
  - They are running from the wolf.
- The same verb can be transitive or intransitive depending on the context:
  - She drives a grey car.
  - She drove to Hartlepool.
- You may see or hear unnecessary prepositions added to transitive verbs, turning them into intransitive verbs:
  - I met Laura for lunch.
  - I met up with Laura for lunch.
- Each tense has several different forms, giving different meanings. It is important that you use the right tense to convey your meaning and that there is agreement between your subject and verb.

Active and Passive Voices

- A verb can be in either the **active voice** or **passive voice**.
- In the active voice, the sentence or clause has a subject which performs the action of the verb:
  - The dog bit the boy.
- In the passive voice, the subject has something done to him / her / it:
  - The boy was bitten by the dog.
- The person or thing that has performed the action is referred to as the agent. In the sentence above the dog is the agent.
- The passive voice is formed from the verb 'to be' and the past participle.
- The active voice is used much more often than the passive voice. There are times, however, when the passive voice is

> **Key Point**
>
> A transitive verb has a direct object. An intransitive verb has no object or an indirect object.

'to meet' is a transitive verb. Laura is the direct object.

'to meet' has been changed to an intransitive verb with two meaningless prepositions before the object. This is poor English.

'The dog' is the subject and 'bit' is in the active voice.

Now the boy is the subject. There is no object.

> **Key Point**
>
> In the active voice, the subject performs the action; in the passive voice, the action is performed on the subject.

better. In the example above the use of the passive voice encourages the reader to focus on the boy.
- The passive tense can create an impersonal, objective tone. Because of this it is useful in formal writing, for example in academic essays or reports:
  - The results <u>were</u> carefully <u>analysed</u>.
  Note that the passive voice does not always require an agent.

Modal Verbs

- When verbs are used to help form tenses, voices or moods of other verbs they are called **auxiliary verbs**.
- When a verb is used to change the mood of a verb it is known as a **modal verb**.
- Modal verbs can alter the tone of your writing.
- 'Can' and 'could' express ability. 'Can' has a stronger, more certain tone than 'could':
  - I suppose we <u>could</u> get to the top.   – We <u>can</u> get to the top.
- 'May' and 'might' can also express possibility:
  - We <u>might</u> get tired.   – They <u>may</u> ask us where we've been.
- 'May' and 'can' are also used to express permission. 'May' is more polite than 'can'.
  - <u>May</u> I have another one, please?   – You <u>can</u> go now.
- 'Must' and 'should' show certainty or obligation:
  - You <u>should</u> wear a raincoat.   – It <u>must</u> be here somewhere.
- In the first person, 'shall' just expresses the simple future but in the second and third person, it is much stronger, implying determination, promise or command:
  - You <u>shall</u> go to the ball.   – We <u>shall</u> not be moved.
- 'Will' works the opposite way round. In the second and third person, it forms the simple present but in the first person, it implies determination, promise or command:
  - I <u>will</u> get there in the end.
  However, the distinction is a subtle one and 'I will' is often used without any such implication.
- Modal verbs are especially useful in persuasive, argumentative and informative writing.
- They can create a polite tone, especially when used with conditional clauses:
  - I <u>should</u> be most grateful, if you <u>would</u> give this matter your full attention.
- They can also help to create a forceful tone:
  - Something <u>must</u> be done about this.
  - Nobody <u>should</u> have to put up with that.

> **Key Point**
>
> Modal verbs work with other verbs to change the mood or tone.

There are two modal verbs in this sentence. The main use of 'would' is to create conditional clauses.

> **Key Words**
>
> active voice
> auxiliary verb
> intransitive verb
> modal verb
> passive voice
> transitive verb

Quick Test

1. Is a verb without an object transitive or intransitive?
2. What is the correct term for the performer of the action in the passive voice?
3. How is the passive voice formed?
4. What sort of clause does 'would' often introduce?

Verbs 2: Revise

Adverbs

You must be able to:
- Understand the function of adverbs and adverbials
- Use adverbs and adverbials accurately and effectively.

Types of Adverbs

- Adverbs modify verbs, giving more information about the action being performed. They can tell us how, where, when or how often the action happens.
- Adverbs that convey how something is done are sometimes referred to as adverbs of manner. These adverbs are usually, but not always, formed by adding 'ly' to an adjective. They can be placed before or after the verb:
  - She performed <u>beautifully</u>.
  - I <u>cautiously</u> approached the door.
- Adverbs of place tell us where the action happens. They are harder to identify as adverbs because they do not end in 'ly'. They are usually placed after the verb but 'here' and 'there' are often used to start sentences:
  - <u>Here</u> we all are.
  - The cows were grazing <u>far away</u>.
  - The bathroom is <u>upstairs</u>.
- Adverbs of time say when something happens:
  - I'm going on holiday <u>tomorrow</u>.
  - <u>Now</u> they're banging on the door.
- Adverbs of frequency say how often something happens:
  - We <u>usually</u> go to Majorca.
  - He brings the milk <u>daily</u>.

Interrogative Adverbs

- 'Why', 'where', 'when' and 'how' are **interrogative** adverbs, which means that they are used to ask questions. After them, the normal order of subject and verb is reversed:
  - How did that happen?
  - When was Henry VII born?
- They can also act as relative adverbs, connecting subordinate clauses to main clauses:
  - He told me where the bus stop was.
  - Nobody knew why they left.

Adverbial Phrases and Clauses

- An adverbial phrase is a group of words used to modify a verb.

> **Key Point**
>
> An adverb modifies a verb.

> **Key Point**
>
> Adverbial phrases and clauses perform the same function as adverbs.

Revise

- Adverbs can be placed before adjectives to modify their meaning. They usually intensify the adjective:
  - You are a <u>terribly clever</u> person.
- Adverbial phrases, like adverbs, can tell us how, where, when or how often the action happens. The only difference is that they consist of two or more words:
  - She left <u>in a hurry</u>.
  - <u>Waving cheerfully</u>, he left.
  - They're moving <u>in a southerly direction</u>.
  - Get it to me <u>before Monday</u>.
- An adverbial clause also modifies a verb, but it contains a subject and predicate so is capable of standing alone as a sentence. It is a type of subordinate clause and it must be connected to the main clause by a conjunction which shows the relationship between the clauses:
  - He was working at the café <u>because he was saving for a car</u>.
  - <u>If it rains</u>, we will stay in.
- Adverbs, adverbial phrases and adverbial clauses are known collectively as adverbials. When an adverbial is placed at the beginning of a sentence, before the main verb, it is called a **fronted adverbial**.

Discourse Markers

- Adverbials can be used as **discourse markers**, which are words or phrases that make connections between sentences or paragraphs and 'signpost' the reader through the text.
- Among the adverbs that are used in this way are 'then', 'therefore', 'however' and 'nevertheless'. These words may be referred to as connectives but they are not conjunctions and should **never** be used within sentences to link clauses. They are used at or near the beginning of a new sentence:
  - I knew I had done well. <u>Nevertheless</u>, I still was not satisfied.
  - In German, capital letters start all nouns. In English, <u>however</u>, we only use them for proper nouns.
- Adverbial phrases and clauses can be used the same way:
  - The workmanship was very shoddy. <u>Because of that</u>, I won't be using them again.
  - The ceremony was very moving. <u>When it was over</u>, we went to the Grand Hotel for the reception.
- For more about discourse markers see page 81.

> ### Quick Test
> 1. What sort of a word does an adverb modify?
> 2. What sort of sentence can begin with an interrogative adverb?
> 3. What does a discourse marker do?
> 4. What is an adverbial called when placed at the start of a sentence?
> 5. Which of these words is not an adverb: however, because, therefore?

Key Words

discourse marker
fronted adverbial
interrogative

Prepositions and Interjections

You must be able to:
- Use a range of prepositions accurately and effectively
- Use interjections appropriately and effectively.

Prepositions

- **Prepositions** are (usually short) words that show relationships between two or more things or people.
- They can deal with relationships in space or time (where or when):
  - I'm <u>on</u> the roof.
  - I've been here <u>since</u> noon.
- They link intransitive verbs to indirect objects.
- They are usually followed by nouns, noun phrases or pronouns:
  - They came <u>from</u> France.
  - She gave it <u>to</u> him.
- Prepositions can consist of more than one word:
  - He's standing <u>in front of</u> the television.
- Some words can be either prepositions or conjunctions:
  - I arrived shortly <u>after</u> you. (preposition)
  - <u>After</u> you left, we played a game. (conjunction)
- Some words can act as either prepositions or adverbs.
  - I'm <u>outside</u> the shop. (preposition)
  - I'm <u>outside</u>. (adverb)
- Prepositions can be used in a non-literal way to express relationships:
  - He thinks he's <u>above</u> everyone else.
  - I'm right <u>behind</u> you on this.

> **Key Point**
>
> Prepositions are used to show a relationship between a person or thing and another.

Using the Appropriate Preposition

- Prepositions are often placed after adjectives. It is important to use the correct preposition with the adjective so that meaning is clear. Make sure you know which adjective takes which preposition. Here are some examples.

Adjective	Preposition	Example
keen	on	He's keen on fishing.
excited happy	about	I was excited about my birthday. I'm happy about your news.
familiar	with	Are you familiar with Dickens?
good	at	She's good at Maths.
interested	in	They're interested in the Romans.
responsible good	for	We're responsible for our own health. It's good for you.
different separate	from	It's different from my last school. I keep the cat separate from the dog.

committed	to	I'm totally committed to the team.
similar		Norway's similar to Denmark.
aware	of	I'm aware of what happened.

- Prepositions can also follow nouns. Make sure you know which preposition should follow which noun.

Noun	Preposition	Example
cause	of	We have found the cause of the problem.
reduction	in	There was a large reduction in cases.
admiration	for	I have a lot of admiration for her.
problem	with	There's a problem with the printer.
advice	on	Could I have some advice on the matter?
answer	to	I don't know the answer to that.

- It is important to use the appropriate preposition when it follows a verb.

Verb	Preposition	Example
persuade	to	I persuaded her to go.
speak		I'll have to speak to the boss about that.
hope	for	I'm hoping for better weather.
know	of	I know of three species.
indulge	in	I like to indulge in a bar of chocolate occasionally.
separate	from	We separated the wheat from the chaff.
concentrate	on	Please concentrate on your work.

Revise

Interjections

- An **interjection** is an exclamation that expresses a strong feeling.
- Interjections can be separated from the rest of the sentence by a comma or can form sentences on their own, punctuated by a full stop or an exclamation mark:
  - <u>Well</u>, I suppose I'll have to accept it.
  - <u>Gosh!</u> That's incredible.
- 'Yes' and 'no' are interjections when they are the replies to questions:
  - <u>Yes</u>, of course I will.
- Interjections are rare in formal writing. Therefore, they are often **slang** words or phrases that go in and out of fashion quickly:
  - Gee whizz!   – Cool.

> **Key Point**
>
> Interjections are informal expressions of strong emotion.

> **Quick Test**
>
> 1. What usually follows a preposition?
> 2. Can a preposition consist of more than one word?
> 3. When are 'yes' and 'no' interjections?
> 4. To what do prepositions link intransitive verbs?

> **Key Words**
>
> interjection
> preposition
> slang

Practice Questions

Verbs

1 Match the tense with the sentence in which it is used.

    a) Simple present   **i)** I'll have painted it by next week.

    b) Present continuous   **ii)** I painted it.

    c) Simple future   **iii)** I had painted it already.

    d) Future continuous   **iv)** I am painting it.

    e) Future perfect   **v)** I'll be painting it before too long.

    f) Future perfect continuous   **vi)** I paint it every year.

    g) Simple past   **vii)** I was painting it all day.

    h) Past continuous   **viii)** I shall paint it tonight.

    i) Perfect   **ix)** I'll have been painting for hours.

    j) Past perfect   **x)** I have painted it.   **[10]**

2 Choose the correct verb in each of the following sentences.

    a) I **have spoken / have spoke** to the class today.

    b) I **did / done** my homework today.

    c) We **have ate / have eaten** there twice.

    d) They **rang / rung** the bell twice.

    e) I **seen / saw** you in the park.   **[5]**

3 Change these sentences from the active to the passive voice.

    a) The gang took all the loot.   _____

    b) I drew that picture.   _____

    c) Alistair is eating the pies.   _____

    d) Rhona hates zoos.   _____   **[4]**

Practise

Adverbs

4 In the sentences that follow identify:

  a) **Two** verbs in the present tense _____

  b) **One** verb in the past tense _____

  c) **One** verb in the future tense _____

  Aled has been here for three weeks but he will be leaving early in the morning. Phew! He is a very nice boy but he can be hard work at times. [4]

5 Underline the adverb in each of the following sentences.

  a) The bird sang sweetly in the tree.

  b) I thought she spoke very convincingly.

  c) We are heading north.

  d) Therefore, it is not advisable to do that. [4]

Prepositions and Interjections

6 Insert the correct preposition in each of the following sentences. Choose from:

        for   with   to   from   of   under   about   off

  a) She's allergic _____ penicillin.

  b) _____ what you've said, I infer you're not happy.

  c) He's feeling _____ the weather.

  d) I had a conversation _____ my sister.

  e) I'm very excited _____ the show.

  f) She's doing it _____ you.

  g) I'm not aware _____ any delays.

  h) I was confused because he kept going _____ the subject.

  i) I wish I could dissuade you _____ that course.

  j) I spoke _____ my sister about it. [10]

Review Questions

Nouns

1 Each of the following sentences includes **two** nouns. Circle them.

   a) Dickens wrote a great many novels.

   b) He wrote some stories especially for Christmas.

   c) Tiny Tim is a very sympathetic character. [6]

Pronouns

2 Each of the following sentences includes **two** pronouns. Identify them and state whether each one is a personal pronoun, a possessive pronoun or a relative pronoun.

   a) He is definitely my favourite author.

   ....

   b) 'A Christmas Carol', which is probably his best-known book, sold millions.

   ....

   c) Who else has read it?

   ....

   d) This is not your copy; it's hers.

   .... [8]

Nouns, Pronouns, Adjectives and Determiners

3 Read the following passage from *A Christmas Carol* by Charles Dickens.

So did the room, the fire, the ruddy glow, the hour of night, and they stood in the city streets on Christmas morning, where (for the weather was severe) the people made a rough, but brisk and not unpleasant kind of music, in scraping the snow from the pavement in front of their dwellings, and from the tops of their houses, whence it was mad delight to the boys to see it come plumping down into the road before and splitting into artificial little snow-storms.

Review

In the extract find:

a) **Eight** adjectives

b) **One** compound noun which is also a proper noun and an abstract noun

c) **Two** compound nouns that are also common nouns

d) **Four** other abstract nouns

e) **Five** pronouns

[20]

Conjunctions

4 Underline the conjunction in each of the following sentences.

a) Because it was getting dark, we left the house.

b) If we're quick we'll get home by nightfall.

c) I've got a map so I shouldn't get lost.

d) I enjoyed the visit despite the cold.

e) They could see us shivering but they did not put the heating on.

f) Keep going until you see the crossroads.

[6]

Sentence Structure 1

You must be able to:
- Understand what is meant by a simple sentence
- Use simple sentences and minor sentences effectively.

Simple Sentences

- It is important that you use a variety of sentences in your writing.
- A sentence starts with a capital letter and ends with a full stop, question mark or (on rare occasions) an exclamation mark.
- A simple sentence consists of only one clause.
- It contains a subject and a predicate, which includes a verb. Sometimes that is all it contains:

    – Angela slept. ← subject verb

- The subject is the person or thing that the sentence is about. It always comes before the verb. In the example above, the subject is a proper noun. It could be any kind of noun or a pronoun. There can be more than one subject.

    – She has slept. ← subject verb

    – The kittens are sleeping. ← subject verb

- The verb can be either active or passive. If it is active, like the examples above, the subject is the person or thing performing the action. If it is passive, the subject is the recipient of the action.

    – She was woken. ← subject verb

- Simple sentences with active verbs often also include an object, a noun or pronoun.

    – Her mother woke her. ← subject verb object

- If the active verb is intransitive the sentence may still include an object but it is an indirect object connected to the verb by a preposition which shows the relationship between the subject and the object.

    – Donna slept in the chair. ← subject verb preposition object

- A passive verb does not have an object but it can have an agent (the person or thing performing the action).

    – Donna was woken by her mother. ← subject verb preposition agent

- You can add as many adjectives and adverbs as you wish: it remains a simple sentence.

> **Key Point**
>
> A simple sentence consists of one clause. It has a subject and one main verb.

Compound Sentences

- A **compound sentence** gives two pieces of information which are connected and are of equal value. By joining what could be two separate sentences into one longer one, we show that the two pieces of information are linked.
- The clauses are joined by **coordinating conjunctions**. The main coordinating conjunctions are 'and', 'but' and 'or':
    - Tom made the tea and ← subject verb object coordinating conjunction
    - I set the table. ← subject verb object
- 'But' is used for contrast:
    - Nina likes roses but Jack prefers carnations.
- 'Or' gives alternatives:
    - We could eat now or we could leave it till later.
- 'Nor' can be used in a negative sentence:
    - He did not get a job nor did he go to college.
- If both clauses have the same subject, the subject can be omitted the second time. It is 'understood' or assumed:
    - We could eat now or leave it till later.
- Pairs of words or phrases such as 'either…or' and 'not only…but also' can be used as coordinating conjunctions.
    - Not only did we visit Madrid but we also took a trip to Seville.
- As with simple sentences, compound sentences can include adverbs, adjectives and prepositions.
- A semicolon can be used instead of a coordinating conjunction to make a compound sentence:
    - Nina likes roses; Jack prefers carnations.

Minor Sentences

- A **minor sentence** is not really a sentence at all as it does not contain a main verb. Minor sentences are also known as **fragments**.
- They are very short and used for effect. They can be answers to questions or exclamations:
    - Yes, of course.   – Oh my word!
- They can be used to create an impact in writing:
    - There, under the leaves. A body.
- They should be used very rarely or they will lose their impact.

> **Key Point**
>
> A compound sentence brings together two clauses of equal importance.

> **Quick Test**
>
> 1. Apart from a verb, what should a simple sentence contain?
> 2. What class of word is used to join clauses and make a compound sentence?
> 3. Which punctuation mark can join two clauses to make a compound sentence?
> 4. What is the alternative name for a minor sentence?

> **Key Words**
>
> compound sentence
> coordinating conjunction
> fragment
> minor sentence

Sentence Structure 2

You must be able to:

- Understand what is meant by complex sentences
- Use complex sentences effectively.

Complex Sentences

- **Complex sentences** are sentences which include more than one clause and where the relationship between the clauses is not equal.
- Complex sentences are used to add more detail to a sentence or organise more complex thoughts around a central idea.
- There are several different ways of forming a complex sentence.

Using Conjunctions

- If two clauses are linked because there is a close relationship between them, a conjunction is used to join them and create a complex sentence.
- This sort of complex sentence looks like a compound sentence.
- The difference is that the two clauses do not have equal value. One is the main clause and the other the **subordinate clause**.
- A **subordinating conjunction** expresses the relationship between the two clauses.
- The relationship can be one of time, place, cause, concession or condition.
- The conjunction introduces the subordinate clause.
- Your choice of subordinating conjunction can radically change the meaning of the sentence:
    - I chose him <u>because</u> he was my friend.
    - I chose him <u>although</u> he was my friend.
    - I chose him <u>so</u> he was my friend.
- If the subordinate clause is conditional and the verb 'to be' is used, the correct form is 'were' regardless of person. This is called the **subjunctive**:
    - If I <u>were</u> rich, I would buy you a car.
- In this sort of complex sentence both clauses, as in compound sentences, retain their internal structure:
    - Keisha left as soon as   ← subject verb conjunction
    - she received the message.   ← subject verb object
- The subordinate clause can come before, after or within the main clause:
    - <u>As soon as she received the message</u>, Keisha left.
    - Keisha, <u>as soon as she received the message</u>, left.

> **Key Point**
>
> Complex sentences can give more information and express more complex ideas than other sentences.

> **Key Point**
>
> When adding extra clauses to a sentence, it is important to ensure that they assist understanding rather than impede it. If a sentence becomes overly long and difficult to follow, split it up into shorter sentences. In your writing you should always aim for clarity.

The second of these sentences implies that the speaker feels that he really should not have chosen his friend. The third sentence implies that the choice caused the friendship and may have been the reason behind the choice.

> **Key Point**
>
> For more about subordinating conjunctions see pages 58–59.

If the subordinate clause stands before or within the main clause, commas are used to separate the two clauses.

- It is possible for a complex sentence to include more than one subordinate clause, each introduced by a conjunction:
  - <u>As soon as she received the message</u>, Keisha left, <u>because she knew it was important</u>.

Using Relative Pronouns

- Subordinate clauses can also be linked to main clauses using relative pronouns (see page 55).
- The relative pronoun indicates that the reader is about to get extra information about the subject or object of the sentence:
  - The castle, <u>which was built in the thirteenth century</u>, has had a violent history.
  - I will be staying with Sian, <u>whose house is near the castle</u>.
- Subordinate clauses introduced by relative pronouns are placed after or within main clauses, but not before them.
- 'Whoever', 'whomever' and 'whatever' can be used in the same way but can begin a subordinate clause before the main clause:
  - <u>Whoever arrives first</u> gets the best room.

Using Participles

- **Participle clauses** are subordinate clauses where the verb is in the form of either the present or past participle.
- They act in a similar way to adverbs.
- Participle clauses do not usually have a subject as they refer to the subject or object of the main clause. The subject is implied:
  - <u>Walking to school</u>, I saw a donkey.
  This is a quicker and neater way of saying:
  - As I was walking to school, I saw a donkey.
- The position of the participle clause is important:
  - I saw a donkey walking to school.
- The past participle is used in the same way as the present participle:
  - <u>Exhausted</u>, I went to bed.
  This usage implies cause:
  - Because I was exhausted, I went to bed.
- If the action of the subordinate clause took place in the past, the word 'having' can be used before the past participle:
  - <u>Having woken up early</u>, I went to feed the chickens.
- It is also possible to add a subordinate clause to a compound sentence, creating a **compound complex sentence**:
  - Because the thunder had woken me, I fed the chickens and collected the eggs early, having first put on my boots.

> **Quick Test**
> 1. What sort of conjunction is used to show the relationship between the main and subordinate clauses?
> 2. How is the subordinate clause separated from the main clause?
> 3. Which of these words cannot be used to introduce a subordinate clause?   which   whom   they

Revise

Key Point
You should try to vary the length and type of sentences you use.

In the previous example, it is clear that the speaker was walking to school. In this example it seems the donkey was walking to school – unlikely but not impossible.

Key Words
complex sentence
participle clause
subjunctive
subordinating conjunction
subordinate clause

Sentence Structure 2: Revise   79

Text Structure: Paragraphs

You must be able to:
- Use paragraphs correctly
- Structure your writing effectively, using paragraphs.

Paragraphs

- Paragraphs break up your writing into manageable parts, making the text easier to follow.
- There is no set length for paragraphs. You should try to vary the length of your paragraphs. Long paragraphs may be used for detailed description or explanation; short ones for impact.

When to Start a New Paragraph

- You should start a new paragraph when you start writing about something new.
- It could be a new topic or idea, moving from one aspect of the subject to another or introducing a different opinion:
  - Another cause for concern is the increasing use of pesticides.
  - Other residents take a different view.
- It might be a change of time, perhaps jumping forwards or going back in a **narrative**:
  - The next day, I understood what had gone wrong.
  - When I last saw her, I was on holiday in Sorrento.
- It could be a change of place:
  - The south of France is also pleasant at this time of year.
- You might want to start a new paragraph when introducing a new character:
  - At that point Jonathan Robinson arrived.
- You must start a new paragraph when you are using direct speech and a new person speaks:
  - 'Best wishes to you too,' she replied.

Opening and Closing Paragraphs

- Opening and closing paragraphs can make a big difference to the effect of a text on readers.
- In a **non-fiction** text the opening paragraph is often used to set out the purpose of the text.
- A newspaper or magazine article, however, might start with an anecdote to 'hook' the reader.
- The closing paragraph of a non-fiction text often summarises the arguments that have been made in the preceding paragraphs and reaches a conclusion.

> **Key Point**
>
> The traditional way of starting a new paragraph is to **indent** the first line. Start a centimetre or two in from the margin. This is usual in most books and in handwritten work. It is still the best way of showing you have started a new paragraph.
>
> Many printed and typed texts leave a line between paragraphs. If you do this, you do not need to indent. Conversely, if you do not leave a line, you must indent.

> **Key Point**
>
> For detailed guidance on punctuating direct speech, see pages 46–47.

- In **fiction** the first paragraph must command the readers' attention, intriguing them and making them want to read on.
- Closing paragraphs in fiction often reflect on what has gone before or tie up loose ends. They sometimes refer back to the beginning of the story. This is known as **circular structure**.

Discourse Markers

- Discourse markers connect sentences and paragraphs. They guide readers through the text, showing how a sentence relates to the previous one, or how a paragraph relates to the previous one.
- They are often used in **topic sentences**, sentences at the start of paragraphs which introduce the subject matter of the new paragraph.
- They can be single-word connectives such as 'therefore' or adverbial phrases such as 'in addition to this'.
- A discourse marker can also be a phrase that picks up on the subject matter of the previous paragraph:
    - This sort of behaviour has become all too common.
- It is not always necessary to start a new paragraph with a discourse marker.
- Discourse markers have many different purposes. Here are some examples.

Revise

> **Key Point**
>
> Paragraphs are used to organise texts. They can vary in length.

> **Key Point**
>
> Discourse markers should be used to guide readers through a text.

Purpose	Discourse marker	Example
To add information or ideas	In addition; as well as; furthermore; moreover; also	Furthermore, there is little evidence to support this idea.
To point out a similarity	Similarly; in the same way	In the same way, cats train their young to hunt.
To introduce a contrasting idea or viewpoint	Nevertheless; despite; however; alternatively; on the other hand	Leo, on the other hand, felt we should go back.
To express cause and effect	Therefore; as a result; consequently; in order to	Many residents, therefore, feel it is time for a new plan.
To give order or to sum up	Firstly; finally; in conclusion; basically	Finally, I would like to thank you all for your interest.
To express passing time	Subsequently; later; as soon as; meanwhile; the next day	Archie, meanwhile, had already made his escape.
To indicate a change of place	Elsewhere; on the other side; further on; beyond	Beyond the village you will find acres of vineyards.

> **Quick Test**
>
> 1. Which two ways of starting a new paragraph are acceptable?
> 2. Should all paragraphs be the same length?
> 3. What are words or phrases that connect paragraphs called?
> 4. In which paragraph might you introduce your subject?
> 5. In which paragraph might you summarise your argument?

> **Key Words**
>
> circular structure
> fiction
> indent
> narrative
> non-fiction
> topic sentence

Text Structure: Paragraphs: Revise

Standard English

You must be able to:
- Understand what is meant by Standard English
- Use Standard English accurately and effectively in your writing.

What is Standard English?

- Standard English is the version of English widely accepted as being correct.
- The use of Standard English ensures that ideas are clearly expressed in a form that can be understood by all readers.
- It is important to use Standard English in all your formal written work.

Dialect and Slang

- **Dialect** refers to variations of English used in different places, whether the different parts of the UK or in other countries where English is widely used. It should not be confused with **accent**, which describes how words are pronounced.
- Dialect includes both words and grammatical constructions that are used in a region but are not Standard English. For example, in many parts of Northern England, people tend to say 'I were' rather than 'I was'. What is generally called an 'alley' can be called an 'entry', a 'ginnel' or a 'jigger'.
- **Slang** refers to language that is informal and often associated with young people. It can change quickly over time.
- Slang words and expressions can identify people as part of a particular group.
- It is unwise to use slang expressions in your written work, not only because your readers may not be familiar with them but also because they might soon be out-of-date.
- With both dialect and slang, it is also possible that the words you use to convey one meaning might have a completely different meaning to your reader. This can lead to confusion and, in some cases, unintended offence.

When Not to Use Standard English

- There are times when it is not only permissible but desirable to use non-standard English.
- If you are quoting someone's words you must quote them exactly, whatever kind of language is used.
- Dialogue, both in drama and prose, should reflect the background of the speaker. The use of dialect and / or slang can make your writing more authentic and immediate.

> **Key Point**
>
> Standard English is the version of English considered correct for formal writing.

> **Key Point**
>
> All the rules and conventions described in this book, particularly in the Grammar section, are designed to enable you to write effectively in Standard English.

- The same applies to stories where you use a first-person **narrator**.
- There are occasions in non-fiction writing, too, where non-Standard English might be appropriate, for example in light-hearted articles aimed at teenagers.

Americanisms and Neologisms

- Language is constantly changing. Words and expressions that were not considered Standard English in the past can soon become acceptable.
- This is especially true of Americanisms and **neologisms**.
- Americanisms are words and phrases that originate in American English. Many have been adopted by UK English speakers and have become common. Examples of this are 'train station' for 'railway station' and the use of 'gift' as a verb. 'He gifted them a new car', has the same meaning as 'he gave them a new car', which is both correct and simple.
- Neologisms are new words, often coined to describe new things or concepts. These can become acceptable or can become outdated.

> **Key Point**
>
> Non-standard forms can be used in dialogue, first-person narratives and very informal non-fiction writing.

Common Errors

- Many common errors come about because of the way the writer speaks. The use of 'of' instead of 'have' ('would of' instead of 'would have', for example) is amongst the worst.
- Another very common error is the 'double **comparative**' or 'double **superlative**'.
- A comparative adjective is formed either by adding 'er', usually for short words, or by placing 'more' in front of the adjective:
  – Their garden is bigger than ours.
  – Our garden is more secluded than theirs.
  You must never use both ('more bigger'). The same applies to superlatives:
  – Their garden is the biggest in the village.
  – Ours is the most secluded.
- Beware of the use of adjectives in place of adverbs:
  – You played amazingly – not 'amazing'
  – I'm very well, thank you – not 'good'
- The use of the wrong participle to form the past continuous is very common:
  – They <u>were sitting</u> in the front row.   – not 'sat'
  – I <u>was standing</u> on the step.   – not 'stood'
- Other common errors include confusion between tenses, the misuse of pronouns and the use of unnecessary or incorrect prepositions. You can find more about these on previous pages.

> **Quick Test**
>
> 1. Why is Standard English important?
> 2. When is it acceptable to use non-standard English?
> 3. What does the use of a dialect tell you about the speaker?

> **Key Words**
>
> accent
> comparative
> dialect
> narrator
> neologism
> slang
> superlative

Practice Questions

Sentence Structure

1 State which of the sentences below is a:

        simple sentence   **compound sentence**   **minor sentence**
                 complex sentence   **compound complex sentence**

a) Gone but not forgotten. _____

b) Although we had talked about it at length, I still had misgivings. _____

c) I went straight there. _____

d) Jenny was there already but Lol had not yet arrived. _____

e) After we had sat down, I told them about my idea and they agreed that it was

    a good one. _____ [5]

2 Turn each of the following pairs of sentences into a compound sentence using a conjunction. Choose from:
        and   **but**   **or**   **so**

a) You could take the left fork. You could take the right fork.

_____

b) I enjoyed the film. I found it a bit too long.

_____

c) We like football. We play as often as we can.

_____

d) I was very tired. I decided to go home.

_____ [4]

Text Structure: Paragraphs

3 What do these discourse markers indicate? Choose from:

      cause and effect   **time**   **place**   **contrast**

          similarity   **additional information**   **order**

a) Nevertheless _____ b) Later that night _____

Practise

c) As a result _____   f) In a similar fashion _____

d) Furthermore _____   g) Once _____

e) Lastly _____   h) A little further on _____

[8]

4 Put the following short paragraphs in the correct order so that the whole passage makes sense.

a) My own interest in chess started many years ago, when I was quite small. Somebody bought me a chess set. Unfortunately, nobody in the family knew how to play.

b) Nevertheless, I went along the following Tuesday. I was delighted to find that the more experienced players were happy to teach us beginners. Since then, I've never looked back.

c) However, I was fascinated by the set and determined to learn the game. I asked all my friends if they could play, but not one of them could.

d) I would like to start by thanking you for inviting me this evening. It really has been an enjoyable and illuminating experience.

e) One boy, however, told me that he had heard that one of the teachers wanted to start a chess club at school. He suggested that we should go along together. I was a little worried that it might not be suitable for beginners.

_____ [10]

Standard English

5 Tick the sentences that are written in Standard English.

a) Be careful not to use too much slang. ☐

b) We ain't never tried that before. ☐

c) I were just wondering what to read first. ☐

d) If she were here now, she would give us good advice. ☐

e) You love that player what scored a goal. ☐   [2]

Review Questions

Verbs 1: Tenses

1 The following sentences are in the present continuous tense. Rewrite them in the simple past.

a) I am going to London.

b) The dog is eating my lunch.

c) They are doing their best.

d) She is ringing the bell. [4]

2 Change the following sentences from the simple past to the perfect tense.

a) I went to the dentist's.

b) She spoke to me about my gums.

c) I brushed my teeth.

d) We left school. [4]

Verbs 2

3 Change the following sentences from the passive to the active voice.

a) The vase was broken by the cat.

b) The snow is being shovelled by George.

c) The bike was being ridden by Asha.

d) Rome was founded by Romulus and Remus.

[4]

Review

Adverbs

4 Form adverbs from the following adjectives.

a) nice ....

b) realistic ....

c) good ....

d) successful ....

e) lazy ....

f) daily ....

g) easy ....

h) polite .... [8]

Prepositions and Interjections

5 Underline the prepositions in the following sentences. Some may contain more than one.

a) I don't want to go to bed yet.

b) It's over there – beyond the oak tree.

c) I was persuaded to go by my aunt.

d) I have seen a lot of strange things.

e) We are fully committed to the task.

f) It's on all the time and it's putting me off my work.

g) It is, without doubt, the best outcome. [10]

6 In each of the following sentences insert the correct prepositions.

a) At the end .... the story the frog turns .... a prince.

b) We were battling .... a strong enemy.

c) I climbed .... the tree and reached the top before coming .... again.

d) We were .... the same class .... the local primary.

e) When we heard the noise we dived .... the table. [8]

Review Questions

Sentence Structure

1 Read the following passage, from *The War of the Worlds* by HG Wells, and answer the questions below.

> A few seconds after midnight the crowd in the Chertsey road, Woking, saw a star fall from heaven into the pine woods to the northwest. It had a greenish colour, and caused a silent brightness like summer lightning. This was the second cylinder.

a) What kind of sentence is the first sentence? ....

b) Identify the main verb in the first sentence. ....

c) What kind of sentence is the second sentence? ....

d) What kind of sentence is the third sentence? ....

e) Identify **five** prepositions.

....

f) Identify an adverbial phrase.

.... [10]

2 On a separate piece of paper, rewrite the following sentences using a participle clause.

a) As I was arriving, I noticed something odd.

b) Because I was surprised, I stopped suddenly.

c) After I had stopped, I took a deep breath. [3]

3 In which of these sentences does the subordinate clause:

a) give the reason for the main clause? ☐

b) give the condition for the main clause? ☐

c) say what happened after the main clause? ☐

d) tell us more about the subject of the main clause? ☐

e) tell us more about the object of the main clause? ☐

Review

    i) If I see it again, I'll let you know.

    ii) I saw an animal, which had whiskers and a long tail.

    iii) I didn't take a picture because I didn't have time.

    iv) Before I went, I had a good look around.

    v) The creature, which had startled me, had gone. [5]

Text Structure: Paragraphs

4 Insert the most appropriate discourse marker in each paragraph so that the whole passage makes sense. Choose from:

in spite of   **days later**   **finally**   **on the third night**   **however**

a) It was _____ when I caught up with Aaron. He told me that he had visited the area several times in search of the mysterious creature. He was determined to find it.

b) It, _____, did not want to be found. He had taken his camera and settled himself down opposite the bushes. Every night he spent two or three hours there.

c) _____ he had heard noises coming from the bushes. It was a growl, he said. It must have been the creature. He did not approach the bushes as he did not want to disturb it, hoping it would show itself. He sat patiently and listened.

d) _____ his patience, it did not emerge. The next night followed the same pattern, as did the the one after that. Each night Aaron recorded what he heard and now he played it to me. We listened. We listened again. We discussed what it might be.

e) _____, I had to agree. It was probably no more than a large, angry domestic cat but I'd still like to see it. Just to be sure. [5]

Standard English

5 Rewrite these sentences in Standard English.

a) Me mind was full of thoughts about me family.

_____

b) He drunk his tea and sunk down into his chair.

_____ [2]

Mixed Test-Style Questions

Spelling and Vocabulary

1 Add a prefix to each of the following words to give them a negative meaning.

a) enviable _____	f) ambitious _____

b) regular _____	g) expedient _____

c) coherent _____	h) perfect _____

d) truthful _____	i) grateful _____

e) precise _____	j) mobile _____ [10]

2 Add a suffix to the following adjectives and verbs to form nouns.

a) command _____	f) anticipate _____

b) electric _____	g) reside _____

c) happy _____	h) minister _____

d) periodic _____	i) free _____

e) loose _____	j) great _____ [10]

3 Read the passage below and identify the word or phrase which is an antonym for each of the underlined words.

Elizabeth said that although she would like to be <u>younger</u> and a bit more healthy, she was <u>content</u> with how life had treated her. She had a lot of friends and saw her children <u>regularly</u>. She was <u>keen</u> to stay fit and would accept any help that was offered.

a) **younger**	youthful ☐	older ☐	old ☐

b) **content**	happy ☐	unhappy ☐	amused ☐

c) **regularly**	frequently ☐	never ☐	occasionally ☐

d) **keen**	reluctant ☐	dull ☐	enthusiastic ☐ [4]

4 Rearrange the letters to form words. There are clues in the brackets.

a) eeltibcyr (star)	c_____

b) ceparpanea (how something looks)	a_____

90　KS3 Spelling, Punctuation and Grammar Revision Guide

Mix it Up

c) jiedtacev (modifies a noun)   a..

d) hanmoylelc (sadness)   m..

e) sorenorich (an animal)   r.. [5]

5 In the following passage replace the underlined words or phrases with the appropriate words from the list below.

| adolescents | attended | considered | a decade | emigrated |
| extremely | fortunate | in retrospect | mundane | remained |

I have known Karl since we were <u>teenagers</u> ....
We <u>went to</u> .... the same school for over <u>ten years</u>
.... Afterwards, he <u>went</u> .... to
Canada and I <u>stayed</u> .... I <u>thought</u> ....
my life <u>very</u> .... <u>dull</u> .... However,
<u>looking back</u> .... , I realise that we have both been very <u>lucky</u>
.... [10]

6 Proofread the passage below, in which there are **five** spelling errors. Circle them and write them correctly below.

Karl returns nearly every year to visit his parents, whos house backs onto ours. Our two families have known each other for genarations. In fact, Karl's farther has done a lot of research and says our ansestors have lived in the same village since medivial times.

a) ....   d) ....

b) ....   e) ....

c) .... [5]

7 Each of the following sentences includes **two** incorrect spellings. Rewrite them, correctly spelt.

a) He was convicted of greivous bodly harm. ....

b) He had onley confessed to recieving stolen goods. ....

c) The judge past sentance on him. ....

d) The victims thort he had got off litely. ....

e) He went to goal for sevaral months. ....

Mixed Test-Style Questions

f) He had denyed everything at first but now he admitted his guilt.

g) He said what happened to him should definately act as a deterent.

h) The events occured in the distant passed.

i) The victim has made a successfull recovery from his ingeries.

j) He is now liveing in a different neighborhood.

[20]

8 Draw lines to match these words with their meanings.

a) constellation   courage in adversity

b) tyrant   lazy

c) anarchy   someone who studies epidemics

d) indolent   not fact

e) fictitious   a type of dance

f) fortitude   lack of order

g) lugubrious   group of stars

h) epidemiolgist   mournful / dreary

i) consternation   worry

j) minuet   oppressive ruler

[10]

9 Put the following words into their plural forms.

a) sandwich   d) phrase

b) graph   e) disco

c) granny   f) man

[6]

Mix it Up

10 Read the passage below and identify the word or phrase which is a synonym for each of the underlined words.

Octogenarian Elizabeth Pritt was among the first residents of Collybourne to receive the inoculation. Afterwards, she declared that the experience had been exhilarating and urged others to follow her lead.

a) **Octogenarian**   seventy year-old ☐   eighty year-old ☐   ninety year-old ☐

b) **Residents**   inhabitants ☐   women ☐   doctors ☐

c) **Inoculation**   medicine ☐   vaccination ☐   prize ☐

d) **Declared**   complained ☐   whispered ☐   announced ☐   [4]

11 Choose the correct word from the pairs in the sentences below.

a) When the fox ran out, the driver had to **break / brake** hard.

b) The lady **led / lead** the group to the hall.

c) The flats were built on the **site / cite** of an old graveyard.

d) He decided to become a blood **doner / donor**.

e) She wrote it all down in her **dairy / diary**.

f) The barrister for the **persecution / prosecution** put her case.   [6]

12 Proofread the passage below, in which there are **five** spelling errors. Circle or underline them and write them correctly below.

The Pritts live in a neat, well-kept bungalow in an unexeptional street just of the main road. Mr and Mrs Pritt have been marryed for over sixty years. When they moved in, there were feilds to the north and east of their home. It is much more built up now and can ocasionally be quite noisy, but they still enjoy living there.

a) ....   d) ....

b) ....   e) ....

c) ....   [5]

Mixed Test-Style Questions

Punctuation

1. Rewrite the following passage inserting full stops and capital letters. Use a separate piece of paper. Do not use any other punctuation.

   the ship was launched in 2010 it is over 220 metres in length and weighs over 50,000 tonnes over the last ten years it has undertaken cruises to all parts of the world on a typical cruise you will find just under a thousand passengers and five hundred crew members some people feel it is a little on the small side but others praise the intimate atmosphere [10]

2. Rewrite the following passage, inserting commas where appropriate. Use a separate piece of paper.

   While some of the larger cruise ships make an effort to appeal to young people the small ones tend to focus on an older market. The *Ariadne* which caters for under a thousand people definitely counts as 'small'. It has a range of facilities including swimming pools bars restaurants and a cinema. However it can seem rather staid and boring to some people. If you are looking for more fun and excitement you might be better off on one of the more modern liners especially those that cruise the Caribbean. There you'll find more family-friendly activities such as rock-climbing treasure hunts games consoles and 'teen-only' discos. [10]

3. Tick the **five** sentences / pairs of sentences that are correctly punctuated.

   a) I really enjoyed the cruise. ☐

   b) Although, my parents were very enthusiastic we were worried that we might be bored. ☐

   c) Colum, my youngest brother, spent most of the time asleep. ☐

   d) Mum persuaded me to try rock-climbing, which was a new experience. ☐

   e) Of course there weren't any rocks, it was a climbing wall so I don't think it really counts as 'rock-climbing'. ☐

   f) Nevertheless, I enjoyed it. I think I might try real rock-climbing one day. ☐

   g) Colum Marcus, and Zara won the treasure hunt, on Monday. ☐

   h) The next day while Colum was still in bed we spent an hour, at the pool. ☐

   i) Colum asked, 'Why do you always do things without me?' ☐

   j) 'Probably because you're rarely awake.' I replied. ☐ [5]

Mix it Up

4 Insert a comma, a semicolon or a colon in these sentences.

a) There was a choice of flavour ___ apple, banana, pineapple, strawberry or toffee.

b) The sun was shining ___ the water was warm

c) Having enjoyed a lemon sorbet ___ I returned to my cabin.

d) I must admit I fell asleep ___ although I had slept until nine.

e) He kept quoting a line from *Macbeth* ___ 'tomorrow, and tomorrow, and tomorrow'. [5]

5 In which **five** of the following sentences are apostrophes used correctly?

a) There were a few other family's with children our age. ☐

b) Marcus's family came from Newcastle. ☐

c) I'd never been to the Caribbean before. ☐

d) Lets' try somewhere else next year. ☐

e) Mexico's supposed to be nice. ☐

f) It's not top of our list. ☐

g) I am attracted by it's culture, though. ☐

h) I collected all the glass's and took them to the bar. ☐

i) All our bags we're packed and ready to go. ☐

j) We've kept in touch with a few other families. ☐ [5]

6 Insert inverted commas in the correct places in the following sentences.

a) What are you reading? Zara asked.

b) I told her it was A Christmas Carol.

c) Well, I must say, she replied, it's hardly the weather for it.

d) I said, We've got exams in school when we get back.

e) The narrator calls Scrooge a tight-fisted hand at the grindstone.

f) I understood what tight-fisted meant but wasn't sure about grindstone. [6]

Mixed Test-Style Questions

7 Tick the **five** sentences which are punctuated correctly.

a) There are two lounges – the Havana and the Miami – where you can relax in the shade. ☐

b) (The *Anastasia*) has recently been refitted. ☐

c) Her favourite flowers are violets, sweet peas and forget-me-nots. ☐

d) Jack and Carrie (Zara's parents) ordered a bouquet. ☐

e) The florist was very-helpful and gave them good advice. ☐

f) He said rose's and carnations were always popular. ☐

g) I wouldn't touch it if I were you – it might bite. ☐

h) Have you ever ordered flowers / wine / chocolates online? ☐

i) Zaras grand-mother was delighted with the party. ☐

j) She said (it was a complete surprise). ☐ [5]

8 Rewrite the following passage using the correct punctuation and layout for direct speech. Use a separate piece of paper.

I'd like to thank all of you for the party Mavis said. It really was a complete surprise. Did you really have no idea, asked Zara. Not a sausage. You lot know how to keep a secret. Well, you knew it was going to be your birthday, Carrie said. And it is quite a big one. Well, yes. Of course, I remembered it was my birthday, Mavis replied, but I didn't expect everybody else to. Oh, Mum, you are daft, said Jack. Why do you think we booked a cruise in the first place? Mavis just laughed and drank her champagne. [10]

9 The following passage contains **five** apostrophes that have been correctly used and **five** that have been incorrectly used. Circle or underline the incorrect ones and write the words without apostrophes below.

Mavis's birthday party was one of the highlight's of our holiday. We'd got to know the Morris's quite well over the previous fortnight and we're flattered to be asked to join their celebration. All the ship's crew seemed to know about it and made a big fuss of her. Carrie's and Jack's children were our best friends on the holiday – we did lot's of things together – and we're planning to keep in touch when we get home.

Mix it Up

a) .... d) ....

b) .... e) ....

c) .... [5]

10 Rewrite this passage so that it is correctly punctuated. Use **six** full stops, **one** exclamation mark, **five** commas, **one** colon, **two** semicolons, **two** dashes and **three** apostrophes. Use a separate piece of paper.

One of the highlights of the trip is an overnight visit to Havana Cubas capital city The culture of this fascinating island one of the jewels of the Caribbean is unique During your stay youll have time to sample many aspects of this culture the crumbling colonial buildings the vintage American cars and passionate Latin dances If you prefer to relax you can take a walk along the seafront The more adventurous among you if you can find the time might want to take a trip into the interior Its a world away from bustling Havana although only a few kilometres away Youll love it [20]

11 **Five** of the following sentences are punctuated incorrectly. Identify them and then rewrite them with correct punctuation below.

a) The captain asked Mavis whether she'd like to join him on the bridge? ☐

b) 'I'd love to,' she said. 'It's very kind of you to invite me.' ☐

c) The day after the party, we set sail, for the Bahama's. ☐

d) Several islands, including New Providence, make up the Bahamas. ☐

e) Apparently it's not far from Florida, I've been there. ☐

f) We did all the usual things, Disney World – Everglades National Park – and just enjoying the sun. ☐

g) I liked Walt-Disney-World / Calum preferred the Everglades. ☐

h) Zara said that she wasn't sure. She'd have to think about it. ☐ [10]

Mixed Test-Style Questions

Grammar

1. Each of the following sentences includes **two** pronouns. Circle them and state whether they are personal, relative or possessive pronouns.

    a) It was the highest peak they had ever climbed. _____

    b) Nobody knew who had been there before them. _____

    c) If you want to know, leave your number. _____

    d) I kept all their addresses. _____

    e) We knew it was ours. _____ [10]

2. Each of these sentences includes **two** nouns. Circle them then state whether they are proper, abstract, common (concrete) or collective nouns.

    a) We went to Paris in the spring. _____

    b) We stayed in a reasonable hotel near the Louvre. _____

    c) That was ideal for the teacher because she loves culture. _____

    d) Our group stuck together on the journey. _____

    e) I preferred the cafés to the art galleries. _____ [10]

3. Look again at the **five** sentences above, in question 2. In each sentence find the subject, the main verb, its direct or indirect object, and a preposition.

	Subject	Main verb	Object	Preposition
a)				
b)				
c)				
d)				
e)				

    [20]

4. Look again at the **five** sentences in question 2.

    a) In sentence **a)**, what is the determiner? _____

    b) Identify and copy the noun phrase in sentence **b)**. _____

    c) Identify and copy the subordinate clause in sentence **c)**. _____

KS3 Spelling, Punctuation and Grammar Revision Guide

Mix it Up

   d) Identify and copy an adverb from sentence **d**). ....

   e) Identify and copy a compound noun from sentence **e**). .... [5]

5 Tick the **five** sentences that are grammatically correct.

   a) The café by the hotel was much more cheaper than the one in the Louvre. ☐

   b) Marcie was well excited for France. ☐

   c) Despite the weather, we enjoyed a boat trip on the river. ☐

   d) I have never seen Mlle Chambreau as happy as she was in Paris. ☐

   e) We was a bit late getting back. ☐

   f) We were worried we might have missed dinner however they were still serving. ☐

   g) The other guests had ate all the fish. ☐

   h) That did not bother Marcie, who is not keen on fish, but I had been looking forward to it. ☐

   i) Given the choice, I would have chosen fish. ☐

   j) However, I'm not a fussy eater and I enjoyed all our meals. ☐ [5]

6 Choose the correct word from the pairs in the following sentences.

   a) I was fascinated **by / with** the *Mona Lisa*.

   b) The meals were different **from / than** the ones at home.

   c) We were hungry **so / therefore** we had a sandwich.

   d) Marcie tripped **over / up** a paving stone.

   e) She was **took / taken** to the hospital.

   f) The doctor told her that she had **broke / broken** her ankle.

   g) She tried **real / really** hard to be brave.

   h) She said, 'I haven't seen **nobody / anybody** for hours.'

   i) Mademoiselle visited as often as she **can / could**.

   j) When she returned, everybody **was / were** happy to see her. [10]

Mixed Test-Style Questions

Read the following passage from *The Wind in the Willows* by Kenneth Grahame and answer questions 7–11.

'Ratty,' said the Mole suddenly, one bright summer morning, 'if you please, I want to ask you a favour.'

    The Rat was sitting on the river bank, singing a little song. He had just composed it himself, so he was very taken up with it, and would not pay proper attention to Mole
5 or anything else. Since early morning he had been swimming in the river, in company with his friends the ducks. And when the ducks stood on their heads suddenly, as ducks will, he would dive down and tickle their necks, just under where their chins would be if ducks had chins, till they were forced to come to the surface again in a hurry, spluttering and angry and shaking their feathers at him, for it is impossible to
10 say quite all you feel when your head is under water.

7 In the text above, find the following:

    a) Two proper nouns

    b) One compound noun that is also an abstract noun

    c) One compound noun that is also a concrete noun

    d) Three other abstract nouns

    e) Three other concrete nouns

    [10]

8 Now find in the text above:

    a) Five adjectives

    b) One adverb

c) **One** adverbial phrase

_____

d) **Three** personal pronouns

_____

e) **Three** possessive pronouns

_____

f) **Three** prepositions

_____

g) **Two** coordinating conjunctions

_____

h) **Two** subordinating conjunctions

_____ [20]

9 In the first **two** sentences (lines 1–3) find:

a) A verb in the simple present tense. _____

b) A verb in the simple past tense. _____

c) A verb in the infinitive. _____

d) A verb in the past continuous tense. _____

e) A participle clause. _____ [5]

10 Look again at this sentence:

> He had just composed it himself, so he was very taken up with it, and would not pay proper attention to Mole or anything else.

a) This sentence includes **two** main clauses and **one** subordinate clause. Which of these terms best describes this type of sentence?

compound ☐   complex ☐   compound complex ☐

Mixed Test-Style Questions

b) Who is the subject of this sentence?

....

c) **One** of the main verbs is in the past perfect tense. Identify it.

....

d) The other main verb is a modal verb. Write it down.

....

e) Write down the subordinate clause in full.

....

f) Is the verb in the subordinate clause active or passive?

....

g) The sentence includes **two** direct objects. What are they?

....

h) There are **three** indirect objects – write down **two** of them.

....

[10]

11 In the first paragraph the writer uses direct speech. Look at it again and tick the sentence below which most accurately changes it to indirect (reported) speech.

> 'Ratty,' said the Mole suddenly, one bright summer morning, 'if you please, I want to ask you a favour.'

a) Mole suddenly said it was a bright sunny morning and he would like Ratty to do him a favour. ☐

b) One bright sunny morning, Ratty suddenly asked Mole if he would please do him a favour. ☐

c) One bright sunny morning, Mole suddenly asked Ratty if he would please do him a favour. ☐

[1]

Answers

Pages 4–5 Review Questions

Spelling
1. a) answer, b) famous, c) library,
   d) minute, e) reign [5]

Vocabulary
1. odd [1]
2. insufficient [1]
3. harshness, abandonment, harmful [3]

Punctuation
1. Did you get there in time? [1]
2. Jo, who is my cousin, lives in the next road. [2]
3. The birds were singing; the grass was green; the sun was in the sky. [2]
4. He bought three apples, four oranges, a bunch of grapes and a banana. [2]
5. Peter's parents live in Paris. Peter's in Pimlico. [2]

Grammar
1. We did really well when we sat those tests. [3]
2. After she had done the shopping, she went home.
   She did the shopping before she went home. [2]
3. I baked bread and I really enjoyed it. [2]
4. stopped [1]
5. noun: song, verb: sang, adjective: beautiful, adverb: enthusiastically [4]
6. because [1]
7. would [1]

Pages 6–13 Revise Questions

Page 7 Quick Test
1. e
2. Blend
3. a) 'c'
   b) 'ee'

Page 9 Quick Test
1. The words sound the same but are spelt differently.
2. People who live in different areas have different accents and so pronounce words differently.
3. Nouns

Page 11 Quick Test
1. Adding 's'
2. Add 's'
3. Old English (or Anglo Saxon)

Page 13 Quick Test
1. Before
2. 'I'
3. Noun

Pages 14–15 Practice Questions

1. a) c<u>au</u>ght, st<u>ay</u>
   b) br<u>ou</u>ght, tr<u>ay</u>
   c) s<u>oo</u>n, d<u>ow</u>nstairs
   d) cr<u>ow</u>d, <u>ou</u>tside
   e) n<u>oi</u>se [10]
2. a) bel<u>ie</u>ve
   b) b<u>ea</u>ch
   c) b<u>ee</u>ch
   d) dec<u>ei</u>ve
   e) rec<u>ei</u>pt
   f) w<u>ei</u>rd [6]
3. a) rough
   b) which
   c) passed
   d) break
   e) reign [5]
4. a) you're, your
   b) They're, their, there
   c) We're, were, wear
   d) It's, its [10]

5.
Singular	Plural
campus	campuses
cello	cellos
crisis	crises
deer	deer
festivity	festivities
formula	formulae (or formulas)
graph	graphs
ibex	ibexes
icicle	icicles
latch	latches

[10]

6.
Root	Word
apprehend	apprehension
bounty	bountiful
conclude	conclusion
encourage	encouragement
flatter	flatterer
implicate	implication
partake	partaking
permit	permitted
revel	reveller
spooky	spookiness

[10]

Pages 16–23 Revise Questions

Page 17 Quick Test
1. Repeating something until you learn it
2. It may allow incorrect spellings
3. Syllables
4. Silent letters
5. The ones that cause difficulty

Page 19 Quick Test
1. Complex and unfamiliar
2. The ones that you have problems with
3. 'ize' and 'ization'

Page 21 Quick Test
1. Sophisticated, ambitious and adventurous
2. Dictionary

Page 23 Quick Test
1. Alliteration
2. Its meaning
3. Irony
4. Oxymoron

Pages 24–25 Practice Questions

1. a) disappear
   b) exaggerate
   c) fiercely
   d) physical
   e) independence
   f) jealousy
   g) mischievous
   h) playwright
   i) separate
   j) sincerely [10]
2. actually, metre, diary, conscience, parallel [5]
3. February, chocolates, unfortunately, presence, voucher. [5]
4. a) bought, brought
   b) practise, practice
   c) infer, imply
   d) affect, effect
   e) lay, lie [5]
5. borrow, principle, queue, discreetly, accepted [5]
6. a) simile
   b) alliteration
   c) hyperbole
   d) assonance
   e) metaphor [5]

Pages 26–27 Review Questions

1. a) mite, might
   b) maid, made
   c) aloud, allowed [3]
2. a) Where
   b) their
   c) we're
   d) there
   e) wear
   f) there
   g) your
   h) They're
   i) were
   j) you're [10]

Answers 103

3.

Singular	Plural
Parry (name)	(the) Parrys
pass	passes
ploy	ploys
raspberry	raspberries
rush	rushes
sheaf	sheaves
ski	skis
turkey	turkeys
veto	vetoes
zoo	zoos

[10]

4. a) ageing
   b) omitting
   c) regretting
   d) neglecting
   e) hesitating
   f) monitoring [6]
5. a) unequal
   b) inoffensive
   c) imperfect
   d) illegible
   e) undefeated
   f) indefensible
   g) ignoble
   h) antisocial
   i) incapable
   j) irresistible [10]
6. Because, break, occasionally, wandered, kilometres, past, churches, exciting, passed, weight [10]

Pages 28–35 Revise Questions

Page 29 Quick Test
1. Full stop
2. Full stop, exclamation mark
3. With a capital letter
4. Comma splicing
5. Surprise, shock, strong emotion

Page 31 Quick Test
1. Yes, if required to make meaning clear
2. When introducing direct speech
3. Relative pronoun, conjunction
4. Subordinate clause

Page 33 Quick Test
1. A list, an explanation, a quotation, direct speech
2. A comma
3. A conjunction
4. Compound words
5. Forward slash

Page 35 Quick Test
1. Brackets
2. With a full stop
3. Dashes

Pages 36–37 Practice Questions

1. It is a short walk from town to our house. The house is built on the side of a gently sloping hill. A blue gate leads to a short gravel path. This takes you to the front door. It is not a particularly attractive house but it is very welcoming. There are two reception rooms and a large kitchen downstairs. A door from the kitchen leads out onto the back garden. Upstairs you will find three bedrooms and a bathroom. From my room there is a stunning view of the river. My family have lived there for over a hundred years.
   [10, 1 mark for each correct example of full stop + capital letter]
2. a) Full stop
   b) Question mark
   c) Full stop
   d) Exclamation mark
   e) Question mark [5]
3. a) There are three bedrooms, a bathroom, two reception rooms and a kitchen.
   b) Ideally, I'd like to have it fully restored.
   c) The local shop, which is about a mile away, doesn't have a wide range of food.
   d) There are, however, a lot more shops in town.
   e) 'I wouldn't sell if I were you,' she remarked.
   f) Old Ben, our nearest neighbour, will be moving in the spring.
   [10, 1 mark for each comma]
4. My grandparents keep a lot of animals: Jemima the horse, who has been with them the longest; Dino the Airedale, who came from a local charity; a three-legged cat called Fred; two guinea pigs without names; and, last but not least, ten noisy but useful brown hens. [5]
5. The correct sentences are: a), c), d), g) and h). [5]
6. a) Gillian (the one who likes horses) lives in the next village.
   b) The Department for Education (DfE) is in charge of national policy for schools.
   c) The guinea pigs – Please don't interrupt me, Giles. – haven't been fed today.
   d) There's only one person responsible for this – you.
   e) My grandma (Mrs Harrison to you) is out at the moment. [5]
   Either brackets or dashes are acceptable for a), c) and e).

Pages 38–39 Review Questions

1. The correct words are: a), e), f), h). [4]
2. science, chemistry, physics, laboratory, assessed [5]
3. a) exclaim, b) retort, c) murmur, d) announce, e) mention [5]
4. a) lose, loose
   b) enquiry, inquiry
   c) compliment, complements
   d) eludes, alluded
   e) uninterested, disinterested
   [5, 1 mark for correct use of each set of words]

6. a) as an ox
   b) Love
   c) angry
   d) sang sweetly
   e) loose cannon [5]

Pages 40–47 Revise Questions

Page 41 Quick Test
1. Use of the abbreviation has become accepted practice
2. One
3. 'is' and 'has'
4. 'd

Page 43 Quick Test
1. 's
2. An apostrophe (')
3. 's
4. No
5. No

Page 45 Quick Test
1. When the quotation fits naturally into the sentence
2. Colon
3. No
4. When there is a quotation, direct speech or a title within a quotation

Page 47 Quick Test
1. Direct speech
2. Comma
3. By starting a new paragraph / line
4. Italics
5. No

Pages 48–49 Practice Questions

1. a) I won't go. b) We can't do it.
   c) That's not yours or That isn't yours.
   d) They're over there. e) She's in the other room. f) I'll not be there or I shan't be there. [6]
2. a) My mother's uncle
   b) Jonny's hamsters
   c) The boss's office
   d) Anna and Samina's friends
   e) The women's room [5]
3. My sister's friend from France is coming to stay with us for a week. She's going to have my brother Tom's room because he's away at university. It took us days to tidy up all his things. Luckily she isn't a fussy eater, according to Lia. I hope she likes pizzas because that's about all Lia will eat. Mum thinks she'll probably need a healthier diet, however, so she went to the greengrocer's today and came back with potatoes, tomatoes, courgettes and some weird looking things I'd never seen before. Lia says I mustn't try to speak to her in French but Mrs Jones says I need the practice. [10]
4. a) Blake uses words such as 'night' and 'dark' to create a sense of danger.
   b) The picture of the child, 'wet with dew', invokes sympathy.
   c) Suddenly the danger is gone: 'And away the vapour flew.'
   d) 'The Little Boy Lost' is a very disturbing poem. [4]

5. **a)** He said, 'Let's go to the cinema.'
   b) 'Would you like a slice of cake?' Mary asked.
   c) 'I would like one', he replied, 'but I'd better not.' [3]
6. The correct answers are: **a)**, **c)**, **d)**, **e)** and **h)**. [5]

Pages 50–51 Review Questions

1. Knowing that we were about to run out of tea and biscuits, I went to the corner shop. It was shut. I had to change my plans and go to the supermarket, which is twenty minutes' walk away. However, I had plenty of time and, besides, I enjoy walking. Unfortunately, by the time I got there I had completely forgotten what I had gone for. [5]
2. **a)** I bought coffee, bread, milk and apples.
   b) As I was approaching the checkout, I bumped into Mo, who lives across the road.
   c) Mo said, 'You haven't got much shopping, have you?'
   d) 'I only wanted tea,' I replied, 'and a packet of garibaldis.'
   e) Mo, a person who thinks life is one big joke, collapsed into helpless laughter. [10]
3. The correct answers are: **b)**, **d)**, **h)**, **i)** and **j)**. [5]
4. **a)** semicolon, **b)** colon, **c)** slash, **d)** hyphen, **e)** colon, **f)** semicolon, **g)** ellipsis, **h)** colon, **i)** ellipsis, **j)** slash [10]
5. **a)** all-knowing, **b)** dog / cat, **c)** Carrington-Brown, **d)** and / or, **e)** eighty-nine [5]
6. **a)** semicolon, **b)** brackets, **c)** colon, **d)** ellipsis, **e)** brackets [5]

Pages 52–59 Revise Questions

Page 53 Quick Test
1. Proper noun
2. Abstract
3. Singular

Page 55 Quick Test
1. Number, person, gender and case
2. You

Page 57 Quick Test
1. Noun
2. Verb
3. The
4. Possessive pronoun

Page 59 Quick Test
1. No
2. Yes
3. Coordinating conjunction
4. Subordinate clause
5. Conditional

Pages 60–61 Practice Questions

1. **a)** wall, **b)** children, toffee, **c)** law, times, **d)** brother, Scarborough, train, **e)** hindsight, thing [10, 1 mark for each noun]
2. **a)** proper and common, **b)** common, **c)** abstract, **d)** common, **e)** proper and abstract, **f)** abstract, **g)** collective and common, **h)** common [1 for each, maximum 8]
3. **a)** she **b)** they **c)** them **d)** her **e)** she and him [1 for each, maximum 6]
4. **a)** lovely, **b)** light, **c)** new, **d)** huge, **e)** grateful [5]
5. **a)** Rollo and I are brothers.
   b) They are great chips.
   c) They sent a present to Jan and me.
   d) They are good people.
   e) We aren't happy today. [5]
6. **a)** and, **b)** If, **c)** because, **d)** Although, **e)** but [5]

Pages 62–63 Review Questions

1. **a)** it's, we've
   b) Ladies', gentlemen's
   c) That's, it's
   d) I'll, class's, I've
   e) family's [10]
2. **a)** Give me your pencil.
   b) We played dominoes.
   c) It's all yours.
   d) There were two failures and eight passes.
   e) I lost my keys.
   f) Dan and Dora's mother's called Doris.
   g) He's left his wallet behind.
   h) I won't be trying that again.
   i) I don't know where I left it.
   j) Joanna's selling pianos. [10]
3. The correct answers are: **b)**, **c)**, **e)**, **g)**. [4]
4. The correct answers are: **a)**, **d)**, **e)**, **f)** and **g)**. [5]
5. **a)** I've just finished reading 'The Lion the Witch and the Wardrobe'.
   b) I asked, 'Would you like to borrow it?'
   c) They are referred to as 'star cross'd lovers'.
   d) She's having what she always calls 'forty winks'.
   e) 'It would be much better,' he said, 'to get a good night's sleep.' [5]
6. The correct answers are: **a)**, **b)**, **e)**, **f)**. [4]

Pages 64–71 Revise Questions

Page 65 Quick Test
1. Simple present and present continuous
2. To be
3. 'ing'
4. 'have' or 'has' + the past participle

Page 67 Quick Test
1. Intransitive
2. Agent
3. By using the verb 'to be' + the past participle
4. Conditional

Page 69 Quick Test
1. Verb
2. Question
3. It connects sentences or paragraphs
4. Fronted adverbial
5. Because

Page 71 Quick Test
1. Noun, noun phrase or pronoun
2. Yes
3. When they answer questions
4. The indirect object

Pages 72–73 Practice Questions

1. **a)** vi, **b)** iv, **c)** viii, **d)** v, **e)** i, **f)** ix, **g)** ii, **h)** vii, **i)** x, **j)** iii [10]
2. **a)** have spoken, **b)** did, **c)** have eaten, **d)** rang, **e)** saw [5]
3. **a)** All the loot was taken by the gang.
   b) That picture was drawn by me.
   c) The pies are being eaten by Alistair.
   d) Zoos are hated by Rhona. [4]
4. **a)** is, can; **b)** has been; **c)** will be leaving [4]
5. **a)** sweetly, **b)** convincingly, **c)** north, **d)** therefore [4]
6. **a)** to, **b)** From, **c)** under, **d)** with, **e)** about, **f)** for, **g)** of, **h)** off, **i)** from, **j)** to [10]

Pages 74–75 Review Questions

1. **a)** Dickens, novels; **b)** stories, Christmas; **c)** Tiny Tim, character [6]
2. **a)** He (personal), my (possessive)
   b) which (relative), his (possessive)
   c) Who (relative), it (personal)
   d) your (possessive), hers (possessive) [8]
3. **a)** ruddy, severe, rough, brisk, not unpleasant, mad, artificial, little
   b) Christmas morning
   c) city streets, snow-storms
   d) hour, night, kind, delight
   e) they, their (× 2), it (× 2) [20]
4. **a)** Because, **b)** If, **c)** so, **d)** despite, **e)** but, **f)** until [6]

Pages 76–83 Revise Questions

Page 77 Quick Test
1. Subject
2. Coordinating conjunction
3. Semicolon
4. Fragment

Page 79 Quick Test
1. Subordinating conjunction
2. By a comma / commas
3. They

Page 81 Quick Test
1. Indentation or leaving a line
2. No
3. Discourse markers
4. Opening paragraph
5. Closing paragraph

Page 83 Quick Test
1. Because it is easily understood by most people
2. Dialogue / speech / informal writing / quotations
3. Where she / he comes from

Pages 84–85 Practice Questions

1. a) minor sentence
   b) complex sentence
   c) simple sentence
   d) compound sentence
   e) compound complex sentence [5]
2. a) or, b) but, c) and / so, d) so [4]
3. a) contrast   b) time
   c) cause and   d) additional
      effect   information
   e) order   f) similarity
   g) time   h) place [8]
4. The correct order is: d), a), c), e), b). [10]
5. The correct answers are: a), d). [2]

Pages 86–87 Review Questions

1. a) I went to London.
   b) The dog ate my lunch.
   c) They did their best.
   d) She rang the bell. [4]
2. a) I have been to the dentist's.
   b) She has spoken to me about my gums.
   c) I have brushed my teeth.
   d) We have left school. [4]
3. a) The cat broke the vase.
   b) George was shovelling the snow.
   c) Asha was riding the bike.
   d) Romulus and Remus founded Rome. [4]
4. a) nicely   b) realistically
   c) well   d) successfully
   e) lazily   f) daily
   g) easily   h) politely [8]
5. a) to…to   b) beyond
   c) to…by   d) of
   e) to   f) on…off
   g) without   [10]
6. a) of, into   b) against
   c) up, down   d) in, at
   e) under   [8]

Pages 88–89 Review Questions

1. a) simple   b) saw
   c) compound   d) simple
   e) after, in, from, into, to
   f) A few seconds after midnight [10]
2. a) Arriving, I noticed something odd.
   b) Surprised, I stopped suddenly.
   c) Having stopped, I took a deep breath. [3]
3. a) iii, b) i, c) iv, d) v, e) ii [5]
4. a) days later, b) however, c) On the third night, d) In spite of, e) Finally [5]
5. a) My mind was full of thoughts about my family.
   b) He drank his tea and sank down into his chair. [2]

Pages 90–102 Mix it Up Questions

Pages 90–93 Spelling and Vocabulary

1. a) unenviable   b) irregular
   c) incoherent   d) untruthful
   e) imprecise   f) unambitious
   g) inexpedient   h) imperfect
   i) ungrateful   j) immobile [10]
2. a) commandment   b) electricity
   c) happiness   d) periodical
   e) looseness   f) anticipation
   g) residence   h) ministry (or ministration)
   i) freedom   j) greatness [10]
3. a) older   b) unhappy
   c) occasionally   d) reluctant [4]
4. a) celebrity   b) appearance
   c) adjective   d) melancholy
   e) rhinoceros   [5]
5. I have known Karl since we were adolescents. We attended the same school for over a decade. Afterwards, he emigrated to Canada and I remained. I considered my life extremely mundane. However, in retrospect, I realise that we have both been very fortunate. [10]
6. a) whose   b) generations
   c) father   d) ancestors
   e) medieval   [5]
7. a) grievous, bodily
   b) only, receiving
   c) passed, sentence
   d) thought, lightly
   e) gaol, several
   f) denied, admitted
   g) definitely, deterrent
   h) occurred, past
   i) successful, injuries
   j) living, neighbourhood [20]
8. a) group of stars
   b) oppressive ruler
   c) lack of order
   d) lazy
   e) not fact
   f) courage in adversity
   g) mournful / dreary
   h) someone who studies epidemics
   i) worry
   j) a type of dance [10]
9. a) sandwiches
   b) graphs
   c) grannies
   d) phrases
   e) discos
   f) men [6]
10. a) eighty year-old   b) inhabitants
    c) vaccination   d) announced [4]
11. a) brake   b) led
    c) site   d) donor
    e) diary   f) prosecution [6]
12. a) unexceptional   b) off
    c) married   d) fields
    e) occasionally   [5]

Pages 94–97 Punctuation

1. The ship was launched in 2010. It is over 220 metres in length and weighs over 50,000 tonnes. Over the last ten years it has undertaken cruises to all parts of the world. On a typical cruise you will find just under a thousand passengers and five hundred crew members. Some people feel it is a little on the small side but others praise the intimate atmosphere. [10, 1 for each full stop + 1 for each capital letter]
2. While some of the larger cruise ships make an effort to appeal to young people, the small ones tend to focus on an older market. The *Ariadne*, which caters for under a thousand people, definitely counts as 'small'. It has a range of facilities including swimming pools, bars, restaurants and a cinema. However, it can seem rather staid and boring to some people. If you are looking for more fun and excitement, you might be better off on one of the more modern liners, especially those that cruise the Caribbean. There you'll find more family-friendly activities such as rock-climbing, treasure hunts, games consoles, and 'teen-only' discos. [10, 1 for each correct comma]
3. The correct answers are: a), c), d), f) and i). [5]
4. a) colon   b) semicolon
   c) comma   d) comma
   e) colon   [5]
5. The correct answers are: b), c), e), f) and j). [5]
6. a) 'What are you reading?' Zara asked.
   b) I told her it was 'A Christmas Carol'.
   c) 'Well, I must say,' she replied, 'it's hardly the weather for it.'
   d) I said, 'We've got exams in school when we get back.'
   e) The narrator calls Scrooge a 'tight-fisted hand at the grindstone.'
   f) I understood what 'tight-fisted' meant but wasn't sure about 'grindstone'. [6]
7. The correct answers are: a), c), d), g) and h). [5]
8. 'I'd like to thank all of you for the party,' Mavis said. 'It really was a complete surprise.'
   'Did you really have no idea?' asked Zara.
   'Not a sausage. You lot know how to keep a secret.'
   'Well, you knew it was going to be your birthday,' Carrie said. 'And it is quite a big one.'
   'Well, yes. Of course I remembered it was my birthday,' Mavis replied, 'but I didn't expect everybody else to.'
   'Oh, Mum, you are daft,' said Jack. 'Why do you think we booked a cruise in the first place?' Mavis just laughed and drank her champagne.
   [10, 1 mark for each pair of speech marks]
9. a) highlights   b) Morrises
   c) were   d) Carrie
   e) lots   [5]
10. One of the highlights of the trip is an overnight visit to Havana, Cuba's capital city. The culture of this fascinating island, one of the jewels of the Caribbean, is unique. During your stay you'll have time to sample many aspects of this culture: the crumbling colonial buildings; the vintage American cars; and passionate Latin dances. If you prefer to relax, you can take a walk along the seafront. The more adventurous among you – if you can

find the time – might want to take a trip into the interior. It's a world away from bustling Havana, although only a few kilometres away. You'll love it! **[20]**
11. The incorrect sentences are: **a), c), e), f)** and **g)**.
    a) The captain asked Mavis whether she'd like to join him on the bridge.
    c) The day after the party, we set sail for the Bahamas.
    e) Apparently it's not far from Florida. I've been there.
    f) We did all the usual things: Disney World, Everglades National Park, and just enjoying the sun. [Semicolons would be acceptable instead of commas.]
    g) I liked Walt Disney World; Calum preferred the Everglades. [A full stop would be acceptable instead of a semicolon.] **[10]**

Pages 98–102 Grammar

1. a) it – personal; they – personal
    b) who – relative; them – personal
    c) you – personal; your – possessive
    d) I – personal; their – possessive
    e) We – personal; ours – possessive **[10]**
2. a) Paris – proper (and common / concrete); spring – abstract
    b) hotel – common / concrete; Louvre – proper (and common / concrete)
    c) teacher – common / concrete; culture – abstract
    d) group – collective (and common / concrete); journey – abstract
    e) cafés – common / concrete; art galleries – common / concrete **[10]**
3.

	Subject	Main verb	Object	Preposition
a)	we	went	the spring	in
b)	we	stayed	hotel	in
c)	that	was	the teacher	for
d)	our group	stuck	journey	on
e)	I	preferred	cafés	to

[20]

4. a) the
    b) near the Louvre / a reasonable hotel (near the Louvre)
    c) because she loves culture
    d) together
    e) art galleries **[5]**
5. The correct answers are: **c), d), h), i)** and **j)**. **[5]**
6. a) by   b) from
    c) so   d) over
    e) taken   f) broken
    g) really   h) anybody
    i) could   j) was **[10]**
7. a) Two from: Ratty; Mole; the Rat
    b) summer morning
    c) river bank
    d) Three from: favour, attention, morning, company, hurry.
    d) Three from: song, river, ducks, friends, heads, necks, chins, surface, feathers, head, water. **[10]**
8. a) Five from: bright, little, proper, spluttering, angry, impossible.
    b) Suddenly
    c) 'one bright summer morning' or 'since early morning'
    d) Three from: I, he, him, they.
    e) His, their, your
    f) Three from: to, on, with, in, under, at
    g) And, or
    h) So, for **[20]**
9. a) please
    b) said
    c) to ask
    d) was sitting
    e) singing a little song **[5]**
10. a) compound complex
    b) He (Ratty)
    c) had just composed
    d) would
    e) so he was very taken up with it
    f) passive
    g) it, attention
    h) Any two of: it, Mole, anything else. **[10]**
11. c) **[1]**

Glossary

abstract noun – a noun that names something you cannot touch, see or hear, such as an idea or emotion
accent – a way of pronouncing words, usually associated with a region or area
active voice – form of verb when the subject is the person or thing performing the action
adjectival clause – a clause that acts like an adjective
adjectival phrase – a phrase that acts like an adjective
adjective – a word that modifies a noun, e.g. by describing it or adding detail
adverb – a word that modifies a verb, often ending in 'ly'
adverbial – a phrase or clause that acts like an adverb
adverbial clause – a clause that acts like an adverb
adverbial phrase – a phrase that acts like an adverb
alliteration – repetition of a sound at the beginning of two or more words
ambiguity – having more than one meaning
antonym – word with the opposite meaning
apostrophe – (') punctuation mark indicating omission or possession
aside – a line or lines addressed directly to the audience in a play
assonance – repetition of vowel sounds within a series of words
auxiliary verb – a verb used with another verb to form tenses etc.

Biblical – relating to the Bible
brackets – ( ) punctuation marks used to enclose additional information etc. that does not fit easily into a sentence

circular structure – a type of structure where the end of a text refers back to the beginning
classical – relating to the ancient civilisations of Greece and Rome
clause – a phrase which could stand alone as a sentence, having a main verb
cliché – an overused word or phrase
collective noun – a singular noun that refers to a group of people or things
colon – (:) punctuation mark used to introduce lists, explanations or quotations
comma – (,) punctuation mark used to separate clauses or items in a list, or to introduce direct speech
comma splicing – the use of commas instead of full stops to divide clauses
common noun – the name of something you can touch, feel, hear, taste or see

comparative – a word that makes a comparison
complex – made up of related parts
complex sentence – a sentence that includes a main clause and at least one subordinate clause
compound noun – a noun made up of two nouns
compound sentence – a sentence that has two main clauses of equal value
compound word – a word that is made up of two or more words
concession – admission or allowance
concrete noun – a noun that names something that can be experienced through the senses
condition – something on which something else depends
conjunction – a word that joins two words, phrases or clauses
connective – any word or phrase that links clauses, sentences or paragraphs
consonant – a letter that is not a vowel
contraction – shortening
coordinating conjunction – a conjunction used to join two clauses of equal value to make a compound sentence

dash – (–) punctuation mark with a variety of uses
definite article – the
determiner – a short word that helps to define a noun
dialect – variety of English associated with a particular region
dialogue – speech / conversation
dictionary – a book that gives definitions of words
diphthong – the union of two vowels to make one sound
direct speech – the actual spoken words, put in inverted commas
discourse marker – a word or phrase used to connect one sentence to another or one paragraph to another, and to show the relationship between them

ellipsis – (…) punctuation mark used to indicate omission
embed – (of a quotation) to put within a grammatically correct sentence
emphatic pronoun – a pronoun, such as 'myself', used for emphasis
exclamation mark – (!) punctuation mark used to end sentences expressing strong feelings

fiction – imaginative writing that is not factual
fragment – a 'sentence' which does not include a verb (also a 'minor sentence')
fronted adverbial – an adverbial phrase placed before the subject and main verb
full stop – (.) punctuation mark used to end sentences
future continuous – a tense that describes an ongoing action in the future ('I will be going')
future perfect – a tense that describes an action that will be completed in the future ('I will have gone')
future perfect continuous – a tense that describes an ongoing action that will have been completed in the future ('I will have been going')

gender – (in grammar) male, female or neuter

homophone – a word that sounds the same as another word but is spelt differently
hyperbole – exaggeration
hyphen – (-) punctuation mark used to join two words together

imagery – the use of descriptive words to paint a picture in the mind
indefinite article – a or an
indent – to start writing a little way in from the margin
indirect speech – speech that is reported rather than quoted
infinitive – the basic form of a verb
interjection – exclamation
interrogative – questioning
intransitive verb – a verb that does not have an object
inverted commas – ('…') punctuation marks used to indicate speech, quotations etc.
irony – when words are used to convey an opposite meaning
irregular – not following rules

metaphor – an image created by writing or speaking of one thing as if it were another
minor sentence – a phrase presented as a sentence but which does not contain a main verb
mnemonic – a way of remembering something
modal verb – a type of auxiliary verb used to change the mood or state of another verb
modify – alter

narrative – story
narrator – a person who tells a story
neologism – a newly coined or invented word
neuter – neither male nor female ('it')

non-fiction – any writing that is not fiction, including factual texts and opinion pieces
noun – a naming word
noun phrase – a phrase which includes a noun and acts like a noun

object – (in the active voice) thing or person to whom something is done
omission – leaving out
onomatopoeia – the use of a word that sounds like what it describes
oxymoron – two contradictory words placed together for effect

parentheses – another word for brackets
parenthesis – part of a sentence that does not fit into its structure easily, perhaps an explanation or aside, usually marked by brackets or dashes
participle – (either present or past) a word formed from a verb and used to form certain tenses or as an adjective
participle adjective – an adjective formed from the present or past participle of a verb
participle clause – a subordinate clause formed around a participle
passive voice – where the subject has the action done to him / her / it
past continuous – tense describing action that continued in the past ('I was going')
past perfect – tense describing action that was completed at a time before the action being described in another past tense ('I had gone')
pathetic fallacy – sort of imagery where either nature is described as having emotions or where literal description reflects the mood of a narrator or character
penultimate – second to last
perfect tense – describing action that was completed in the past ('I have gone')
personal pronoun – I / you / he / she / it / we / they / him / her / us / they
personification – a type of imagery where an inanimate object or an idea is given human qualities
phrase – a group of words
plural – more than one
possession – belonging
possessive pronoun – a pronoun that shows belonging
predicate – the remainder of a sentence, including the verb, after the subject
prefix – letters that are put in front of an existing word to change its meaning
preposition – a (usually short) word in front of a noun that shows the relationship between the noun and another word

pronoun – a short word used as a substitute for a noun or noun phrase
proper noun – a noun which names a particular thing or person and which starts with a capital letter
prose – any writing that is not verse

quantifier – a determiner that indicates amount
question mark – (?) punctuation mark used to end questions
quotation – words taken directly from another text
quotation marks – inverted commas, especially when used around quotations

received pronunciation – the accent that is the equivalent of Standard English
reflexive pronoun – a pronoun, such as 'myself', used as the object
relative pronoun – a pronoun that introduces a clause, e.g. 'who'
reported speech – another term for indirect speech
rhetorical question – a question which does not require an answer
root word – the basic word to which prefixes or suffixes might be added

semicolon – (;) punctuation mark used to show a close relationship between two clauses or to separate items in a list
sibilance – alliteration of 's' sounds
silent letter – a letter which is not clearly pronounced
simile – a kind of imagery which compares one thing to another using 'like' or 'as'
simple future – the basic future tense ('I will go')
simple past – the basic past tense ('I went')
simple present – the basic present tense ('I go')
singular – one
slang – very informal, non-standard language

solidus – (/) alternative term for a forward slash
speech marks – another term for inverted commas, when used to punctuate speech
strategy – plan
stress – emphasis
subject – when the active voice is used, the person or thing who does something; when the passive voice is used the person or thing who has something done to her / him / it
subjunctive – a form of a verb expressing wish or mood, usually after 'if'
subordinate clause – a clause in a complex sentence which is dependent on the main clause
subordinating conjunction – a conjunction that introduces a subordinate clause
suffix – letters placed after a root word to change its meaning
superlative – expression of the highest degree ('most')
syllable – a single unit of speech
symbolism – a sort of imagery where an object represents an idea or emotion
synonym – a word which has a very similar meaning to another word

thesaurus – a book containing lists of words that are associated with each other, including synonyms
topic sentence – a sentence at the beginning of a paragraph that introduces its theme
transitive verb – a verb that has a direct object

verb – a doing, thinking, feeling or being word
verse – poetry
virgule – (/) an alternative term for a forward slash
vocabulary – word usage
vocalisation – saying something aloud
vowel – a, e, i, o, u

Notes

Index

A
Abbreviations 29
Abstract nouns 53
Accent 6
Active voice 66
Adjectival phrases 31
Adjectives 56–57
Adverbials 30, 68–69
Adverbs 30, 68–69
Alliteration 22
Alternative spellings 19
Americanisms 83
Antonyms 20–21
Apostrophes 40–41, 42–43
Articles 57
Assonance 22
Auxiliary verbs 67

B
Brackets 34

C
Clichés 21
Collective nouns 53
Colons 32
Comma splicing 28
Commas 28, 30–31
Common nouns 53
Commonly misspelt words 18–19
Comparatives 83
Complex sentences 78–79
Compound nouns 52–53
Compound sentences 77
Compound words 33
Conjunctions 58–59, 78
Contractions 40
Coordinating conjunctions 58, 77

D
Dashes 34–35
Determiners 57
Dialect 82
Dialogue 40
Dictionary 16, 20
Diphthong 6
Direct speech 31, 46
Discourse markers 69, 81

E
Ellipsis 35
Embedded quotations 44
Emphatic pronouns 55
Exclamation marks 28–29

F
Fragments 28, 77
Full stops 28
Future tense 64–65

H
Homophones 8–9
Hyperbole 23
Hyphens 33

I
Imagery 22–23
Infinitive 64
Informal negatives 40
Interjections 71
Interrogative adverbs 68
Intransitive verbs 66
Inverted commas 31, 44–45, 46–47
Irony 23
Irregular plurals 11

L
Linguistic techniques 22–23
Long vowel sounds 6

M
Main clause 28
Metaphor 23
Minor sentences 77
Mnemonics 17
Modal verbs 41, 67

N
Neologisms 83
Noun phrases 53
Nouns 52–53

O
Object 76
Omission 40
Onomatopoeia 22
Oxymoron 23

P
Paragraphs 80–81
Parenthesis 34–35
Participle 79
Participle adjectives 56
Passive voice 66
Past tense 65
Pathetic fallacy 23
Personal pronouns 54
Personification 23
Plurals 10–11

Possession 42–43
Possessive pronouns 43, 55
Predicate 28
Prefixes 12
Prepositions 70–71
Present tense 64
Pronouns 40, 54–55
Proper nouns 10, 52

Q
Question marks 29
Quotations 32, 44–45

R
Received pronunciation 6
Reflexive pronouns 55
Relative pronouns 31, 55, 79
Repetition 22
Reported speech 46
Rhetorical questions 29
Root words 12–13

S
Semicolons 32–33
Sentences 28, 76–77, 78–79
Sibilance 22
Silent letters 16–17
Simile 22–23
Simple sentences 76
Slang 71, 82
Slashes 33
Specialist words 19
Speech marks 44–45, 46–47
Spelling strategies 16–17
Standard English 82–83
Subject 28–29, 76
Subjunctive 78
Subordinate clauses 31, 78–79
Subordinating conjunctions 58–59, 78
Suffixes 12–13
Superlatives 83
Syllables 12
Symbolism 23
Synonyms 20–21

T
Tense 64
Thesaurus 20
Topic sentences 81
Transitive verbs 66

V
Verbs 64–65, 66–67
Vowels 6–7

Collins

KS3
Spelling, Punctuation & Grammar

Workbook

Paul Burns

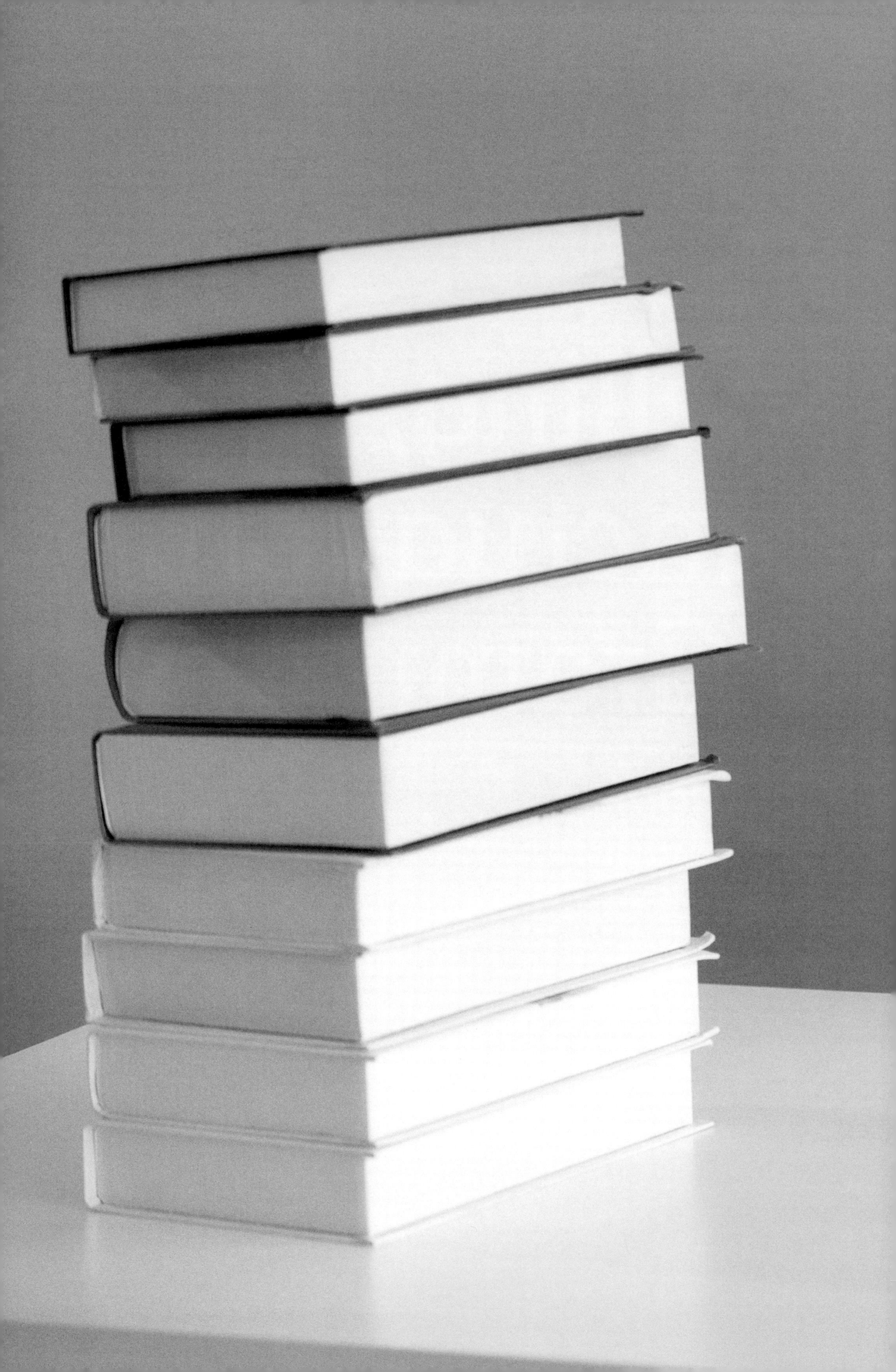

Contents

Spelling and Vocabulary

- 116 Vowels
- 117 Homophones
- 118 Forming Plurals
- 119 Prefixes
- 120 Suffixes
- 121 Spelling Strategies
- 122 Complex and Irregular Words
- 123 Proofreading
- 124 Extending Your Vocabulary
- 125 Using Your Vocabulary Creatively 1
- 126 Using Your Vocabulary Creatively 2

Punctuation

- 127 Ending Sentences
- 128 Commas
- 130 Colons, Semicolons, Hyphens and Slashes
- 131 Parenthesis and Ellipsis
- 132 The Apostrophe for Omission
- 133 The Apostrophe for Possession
- 134 Inverted Commas 1: Quotation and Titles
- 135 Inverted Commas 2: Punctuating Speech

Grammar

- 136 Nouns
- 137 Pronouns
- 138 Adjectives and Determiners
- 139 Conjunctions
- 140 Verbs 1: Tenses
- 141 Verbs 2
- 142 Adverbs
- 143 Prepositions and Interjections
- 144 Sentence Structure 1
- 145 Sentence Structure 2
- 146 Text Structure: Paragraphs
- 148 Standard English

10-Minute Spelling, Punctuation and Grammar Tests

- 150 Test 1
- 152 Test 2
- 154 Test 3
- 156 Test 4
- 158 Test 5
- 160 Test 6

- 163 Answers

Spelling

Vowels

1 Complete the table below with correctly spelt words that include long vowel sounds.

	Long Vowel Sound	Meaning	Word
a	'Oi' as in 'loin'	a robot or phone	a
b	Long 'o' sound as in 'so'	part of a skeleton	b
c	'Oi' as in 'loin'	money	c
d	'Ai' as in 'fair'	state confidently	d
e	Long 'a' as in 'pay'	teach	e
f	Long 'i' as in 'light'	terror	f
g	'Ow' sound as in 'loud'	another word for a dress	g
h	'Ow' sound as in 'loud'	dog	h
i	Long 'u' as in 'sure'	not clean	i
j	'Au' sound as in 'caught'	a pleasure trip	j
k	Long 'i' as in 'light'	a 'sir'	k
l	Long 'a' as in 'pay'	… an egg or a table	l
m	Long 'u' as in 'sure'	grown up	m
n	Long 'o' as in 'moon'	the middle of the day	n
p	'Ai' as in 'fair'	two	p
r	Long 'a' as in 'pay'	a sort of race	r
s	'Ai' as in 'fair'	left over	s
t	'Oi' as in 'loin'	plaything	t
y	Long 'o' as in 'moon'	a young person	y
z	Long 'o' as in 'moon'	the study of animals	z

[20]

2 Here is a list of words that include 'ee' sounds, using 'ee', 'ea', 'ie' or 'ei'. The diphthongs have been omitted. Complete the words.

ach_ _ve   def_ _t   misch_ _f   rec_ _pt

bel_ _f   gr_ _ve   perc_ _ve   s_ _ge

c_ _ling   h_ _ve   pl_ _d   sl_ _ve

conc_ _t   ind_ _d   pr_ _n   tw_ _d

dec_ _ve   kn_ _d   proc_ _d   w_ _ver   [20]

Total Marks _____ / 40

Workbook

Homophones

1 Below are **four** pairs of homophones. Using a dictionary, find out the meaning of each word and write it down.

a) allusion

_____

illusion

_____

b) alms

_____

arms

_____

c) aural

_____

oral

_____

d) bazaar

_____

bizarre

_____

[8]

2 Circle the correct words from the pairs of homophones in the sentences below.

a) They sailed around the **buoy / boy** and back into the harbour.

b) In Belgium we had **muscles / mussels** and chips.

c) We listened to his wise **council / counsel**.

d) After the main course we had strawberry **moose / mousse**.

e) I eat everything I'm given because I don't like **waist / waste**.

f) I'm afraid you're a **cereal / serial** offender.

[6]

Total Marks _____ / 14

Spelling 117

Spelling

Forming Plurals

1 Put these words into their plural form.

a) alloy .... jockey ....

authority .... monopoly ....

blueberry .... opportunity ....

dairy .... quay .... [8]

b) duchess .... manifesto ....

glitch .... mosquito ....

impresario .... pagoda ....

polish .... stopwatch .... [8]

c) crisis .... person ....

hippopotamus .... quiz ....

index .... soliloquy ....

knife .... stratum .... [8]

2 The following passage does not make sense because all the nouns are in their singular forms but the verbs and pronouns are plural. Underline all the **nouns**. Then rewrite the plural forms of the nouns below.

The child were in the field minding the sheep. They were wearing warm coat and wellington boot because it was quite cold and had been raining. All the man and woman had stayed in their house. There were many task to do: washing the dish, mopping the floor, polishing shoe, and feeding the goose. Their offspring suspected they were doing none of these, but were sitting on their patio eating sandwich, pizza and tomato. Still, the boy and girl preferred being outside.

[20]

Workbook

Prefixes

1 Match the prefixes with their meanings by drawing lines between them.

Prefix	Meaning
auto	across
extra	after
inter	again
intra	before
mega	beyond
post	between
pre	half
re	self
semi	under
sub	very big
trans	within

[11]

2 Add **one** of the prefixes in the list in question 1 to each of the root words in the following sentences to give the required meaning.

a) The World Cup is an _____ national competition.

b) The match has been _____ poned until June.

c) The *Queen Elizabeth II* is a _____ atlantic liner.

d) I can _____ dict what will happen next.

e) We all live in a yellow _____ marine.

f) I might have to _____ sit my exams in November.

g) You don't have to do anything: it's completely _____ matic.

h) I've already used 500 _____ bytes.

i) They gave her an _____ venous injection.

j) The children sat around their teacher in a _____ circle.

k) I don't believe _____ terrestrials have visited Earth.

[11]

Total Marks _____ / 22

Spelling

Spelling

Suffixes

1 Form both the present participle and the past participle of these words, using the suffixes 'ing' and 'ed'.

Root Word	Present Participle	Past Participle
benefit		
delay		
edit		
imply		
intensify		
regret		
torpedo		
underline		

[16]

2 Circle or underline the correctly spelt noun(s) formed from the root word.

a) **parent**   parenthood   parentness   parenticity

b) **happy**   happyness   happyhood   happiness

c) **elastic**   elasticness   elasticity   elasticicity

d) **entire**   entirety   entirty   entry   [4]

3 Form a noun from each of the following verbs, using 'tion', 'sion', 'ence' or 'ance'.

a) compete _____   f) extort _____

b) reminisce _____   g) identify _____

c) remember _____   h) neglect _____

d) prescribe _____   i) deceive _____

e) commend _____   j) remit _____   [10]

Total Marks _____ / 30

Workbook

Spelling Strategies

1
- Get out your exercise books and any exam papers you completed in the last year.
- Make a list of the correct spellings of all the words you spelt incorrectly.
- Put an asterisk (*) by any words that you have spelt incorrectly more than once.
- While you are doing this, see if you can discover any patterns. For example, do you tend to make errors with plurals or with homophones?
- If your list is long, select the words that you have spelt wrongly most often and those that you think you are most likely to use again.
- Look at the spelling strategies described on pages 16–17 of the Revision part of this book to see if they can be of use.
- Learn a few spellings every day, using 'look, say, cover, write, check'.
- If you can, ask someone to test you on your spelling words.

2 Look again at pages 16–17 of the Revision part of this book. Copy out any of the mnemonics that you find helpful.

3 Use the boxes below to sketch designs for posters illustrating these mnemonics. Then make the posters and put them up somewhere where you will see them often.

Spelling

Spelling

Complex and Irregular Words

1 Circle or underline the correctly spelt version of the following words.

   a) bissness   buisness   business

   b) chronilogical   chronological   cronalogical

   c) conscence   conscience   consience

   d) exagerrate   egsagerate   exaggerate

   e) alliteration   allitteration   alitteration

   f) developpment   development   developement

   g) unfortunately   unfortunitely   unfortunatly   [7]

2 Circle the correctly spelt word from the alternatives given.

   a) We had to stand in a long **que / queue** to get our tickets.

   b) It was a very **vicious / viscious** little animal.

   c) I fainted and lost **consciousness / conscienceness**.

   d) Art can be very **fulfilling / fullfilling**.

   e) **Possession / posesion** is nine-tenths of the law.

   f) I know I could improve if I had more **discipline / dissipline**.

   g) **Onomatopoeia / Onamatapoeia** is very effective in poetry.   [7]

3 In each group of **three** spellings, **two** are acceptable. Put a line through the **one** that is not.

   a) acknowledgement   acknoledgement   acknowledgment

   b) auntie   antie   aunty

   c) co-operative   cooperative   coperative

   d) dasptach   dispatch   despatch

   e) focused   focussed   foscused

   f) homogenise   homogenize   hommogenise

   g) jail   jaol   gaol   [7]

Total Marks _____ / 21

Workbook

Proofreading

Each of the passages below contains **ten** words that are spelt incorrectly. Underline or circle the errors. Then write them correctly below.

1) The Bloxham family has been bekeing bread for over a century. In that time, their have been many changes in there industry. Many family's like the Bloxhams have gone out of bissness because of competition from the large bakerys and the supermarkets. Bloxham's Bakery, however, has survived into the twenty-first century and is now benefitting from the fashion for 'artisan' bread, especially holemeal loafs and sourdough breads. They provide a wide variety of buns and cakes, from jam doughnuts to merangs.

[10]

2) I have always wanted to be a doctor. I used to borrow my grandfather's themometer and take the temprature of all my toys. I would then drive them in an (imaginery) ambulance to the accident and emergensy department of the nearest hospital (our kitchen table). Once we got there, it was almost inevitable that Teddy would be diagnosed with a condition that recquired an imeddiate operation. Fortunitely for Teddy, I could not perform an amputation as I was not allowed sharp sissors, being under five at the time. Later, I realised that there was a bit of a problem with my ambition when I was given an innoculation in school and instantly feinted.

[10]

3) In the early nineteenth century, the Crown was a simple country pub, caterring mainly for local agriculturel workers, traveling tradesmen or hawkers, and the occasional merchant or gentleman. It was not on a main root to anywhere and did not attract a lot of passing trade. That is not to say it was not busy, however, as it was well-used by the local farmers and laborers, especially at haymakeing and harvest time. As well as the inn, John Woolley rented outbildings and pasteur from his landlord, probably keeping a cow, a pig or two, and poltry.

[10]

Total Marks / 30

Vocabulary

Extending Your Vocabulary

1 In the passage below **ten** words have been highlighted. Use a thesaurus to find words that make the description more precise and interesting. Write the correctly spelt words below.

The **old** man was **walking** down the street, minding his own business. Suddenly he saw something **odd** in the distance. Then he heard a **noise**, coming from the same place. He **moved** towards it. By the time he got there, whatever it was had **gone**. **Tired**, he sat on a **seat** under a **big** **tree**. Then he saw it again.

[10]

2 Use a dictionary to find out the meaning of the following **five** words. Write each meaning below.

a) compromise

b) consensus

c) existential

d) hazardous

e) impediment   [5]

3 This passage contains **ten** words that are used incorrectly. Underline or circle the errors. Then write the correct words below.

Sometimes people come to me, in my roll as principle of the college, and wish to discuss personal issues. It is important, therefore, that they can count on me to be discrete. I have had less of these meetings recently. I hope that this is the affect of the policies we have recently put in place to compliment our existing guidelines, and not because students think that I am disinterested in their problems. Please do not imply from this that I am in any way complaisant about pastoral matters. I am always willing to except justifiable criticism.

[10]

Total Marks _____ / 25

Workbook

Using Your Vocabulary Creatively 1

1 Find a newspaper or magazine, either a hard copy or online. Skim-read it to find examples of each of the following language techniques. Write each example below.

   a) Alliteration

   b) Metaphor

   c) Simile

   d) Onomatopoeia

   e) Personification

   [5]

2 a) Create a headline, using alliteration, about someone called Dan.

   b) Using sibilance, complete this sentence using at least **four** more words.

   Softly

   c) Complete this sentence with a simile.

   Jody arrived

   d) Create a sentence which personifies fear.

   Fear

   e) Use hyperbole to express the emotions of the subject of this sentence.

   Yusuf said that [5]

Total Marks / 10

Vocabulary

Vocabulary

Using Your Vocabulary Creatively 2

1 Write a short (100–200 words) description of a place near where you live or somewhere you have recently visited. Use at least **four** of the following language techniques:

alliteration	assonance	metaphor	onomatopoeia
oxymoron	pathetic fallacy	personification	simile

[8]

Total Marks .... / 8

Punctuation

Ending Sentences

1 Complete the following sentences, using a full stop, question mark or exclamation mark.

a) I got up at eight o'clock this morning

b) Sam asked me if I was feeling all right

c) What a cheek

d) How am I supposed to revise with all that commotion

e) Where we live there is a lot of building going on

f) Where was the noise coming from

g) I haven't got a clue

h) Sam wasn't sure whether to go out or not [8]

2 Punctuate the following passage, using **ten** capital letters, **seven** full stops, **two** question marks and **one** exclamation mark.

What is the point of exams it's a subject everyone seems to have an opinion on my english teacher thinks they're the only fair way of assessing progress but the music teacher disagrees she believes in coursework she thinks the exam boards should base their marks on the teachers' assessments what if the teachers cheated by giving all their students top marks she says it wouldn't happen the english teacher says it happens all the time wow I never thought I'd hear a teacher say that [20]

3 Tick the **two** sentences or pairs of sentences that are correctly punctuated.

A I asked Uncle Jack. He said that exams prepare you for the real world. ☐

B Sam asked him. What he meant by the real world. ☐

C 'The real world? Work!' ☐

D In reply, he told me a long story! About when he left school and was apprenticed to a plumber! ☐

E I couldn't see how that was relevant? ☐

F How can reading old plays and poems help you with plumbing. ☐ [2]

Total Marks _____ / 30

Punctuation

Commas

1 Each of the following sentences should include **two** commas. Insert them in the correct places.

a) She told me she had visited Lanzarote Tenerife La Palma and Gran Canaria.

b) She was so tired that after she got home she went straight to bed.

c) In the morning she phoned Bert Lucy and me.

d) She did not however speak to Pat.

e) I said 'Jan how nice to hear from you.'

f) Very kindly she treated us all to a long leisurely lunch.

g) There was an amazing spread: chicken ham various salads and wonderful desserts.

h) She said 'I think Gran Canaria was my favourite although I do love Tenerife.'

i) I was torn between blackberry and apple pie lemon and mango sorbet and cheesecake.

j) 'On the way back' she said 'I sat next to a really interesting person.' [20]

2 Tick the **five** sentences that are correctly punctuated.

A   Eventually, someone broke the silence.

B   It was Lucy, she said that she would miss Pat terribly.

C   Then we all joined in, some more convincingly than others.

D   Bert said that, when he was in Australia, someone had offered him a job.

E   Pat asked 'Why didn't you take it?'

F   'Because I'd miss you lot,' he joked.

G   Pat, Lucy, Jan, and I groaned.

H   Bert, however, claimed that he had been serious.

I   Then, he admitted, that he would have stayed, but he couldn't get a visa.

J   He had said his brother who was five years older was hoping to go there next year. [5]

Workbook

3 In the following passage **ten** commas have been used incorrectly. Circle or underline them. Then rewrite the passage with correct punctuation, using only commas and full stops.

Of course, when Pat returned, she too wanted to tell everyone about her holiday. She had been away longer than anyone else, she had been to Australia. She told us, the reason she went there was that she had family, out there. There was Uncle Barry, Aunty Beryl, Aunty Lynn, the newly weds Laurie, and Jason, and lots of other cousins. She said she got on with all of them, they were really friendly, they welcomed her with open arms. Bert, who had been there, wondered if, Pat would ever consider emigrating to Australia. She thought for a bit, then she said, 'No, I think I'd miss home too much,' I think she was waiting for someone to say we'd miss her, when nobody did, she looked a bit put out and ate her raspberry, ripple in silence.

[20]

Total Marks / 45

Punctuation

Colons, Semicolons, Hyphens and Slashes

1 Place either a colon or a semicolon in the correct place in each of these sentences.

   a) Malcolm urges Macduff to avenge his family 'Dispute it like a man.'

   b) There were five possible options history, geography, RE, French and science.

   c) I have already read it I'm sending it back.

   d) Gerry decided to buy the picture it reminded him of home.

   e) The Vikings approached from the west the Saxons came from the south. [5]

2 Add **two** colons and **three** semicolons in the correct places.

   I noticed the advertisement at once 'House contents for sale bedroom furniture all kitchen fittings dining tables and chairs and a comfortable three-piece suite.' [5]

3 Place either a hyphen or a slash (solidus), as appropriate, in the correct place in each of these sentences.

   a) Any pupil needing a new bus pass should forward his her details to the office.

   b) I've got boxes of what claimed to be non stick pans.

   c) He came fully equipped with a fountain pen, a new ring binder and plenty of paper.

   d) Sadly, 'all the king's horses and all the king's men couldn't put Humpty together again.'

   e) Olivia Newton John and John Travolta starred in 'Grease'. [5]

4 Tick the **three** sentences that are correctly punctuated.

   A Be careful with that vase: it's fragile.

   B The area is well-served by public transport: buses, trains and ferries.

   C I bought the desk; and the chair.

   D You can-not be serious.

   E It should be here soon: it's been pre-ordered. [3]

Total Marks _____ / 18

Workbook

Parenthesis and Ellipsis

1 Each of the following sentences contains extra information that can be put into parenthesis. Do this by inserting brackets in the appropriate places.

   a) Constantine Rumbold Con to his friends lives in number 19.

   b) Number 21 the big house with the bay windows belongs to the Ahmed family.

   c) At the top of our street Did I mention that I live there too? is an empty property called The Birches.

   d) Mr and Mrs Allenby and their three children Angus, Amanda and Ariadne used to live there.

   e) Ariadne Allenby 18 is at university now. [5]

2 a) Replace the ellipsis in this sentence with the phrase out of the **three** below that makes sense.

   Angus … _____ was in my class at school.

   A and Amanda   **B** has gone to Belfast because   **C** , the Allenbys' son,   [1]

   b) Replace the words in the square brackets with the phrase out of the **three** below that makes most sense.

   Not long ago I heard that [the Birches] _____ had a new tenant.

   A Angus and Amanda   **B** their house   **C** number 19   [1]

   c) Replace the ellipsis in this sentence with the phrase out of the **three** below that makes sense.

   I stood outside the Birches and I wondered… _____

   A but then I went home   **B** what would happen to the house

   C what was for tea   [1]

   d) Place **two** dashes in the following sentence as an alternative to brackets.

   Angus Allenby he's the boy I was telling you about wrote to me about his new school. [2]

Total Marks _____ / 10

Punctuation   131

Punctuation

The Apostrophe for Omission

1 Rewrite this passage, making it less formal by including **ten** examples of the apostrophe of omission.

We are all in this together. We should not be standing on the sidelines watching what is happening from a distance. It is our future they are deciding on. Let us get in there and put our point of view. Maybe they will not listen. That is a chance we must take. One thing I can tell you: they cannot listen if we do not say anything.

[10]

2 Which **five** of the following sentences are correctly punctuated?

A Nobody ever listen's to me.

B You know thats not true.

C I don't really have a strong opinion about it.

D That's all right: I just want to know what you think.

E It's a complicated issue.

F I've found, over the years, that most issues are complicated.

G I'd be grateful if you'd give me a bit more time to think.

H I wiln't be able to, I'm afraid.

I I know were being asked for our views, but in the end its their decision.

J They'll do whatever they wan't; they alway's do.

[5]

Total Marks _____ / 15

Workbook

The Apostrophe for Possession

1 Which **five** of the following sentences are correctly punctuated?

A Who's shoes are those? ☐

B I need a new pair of glasses'. ☐

C A piano's keys are black and white. ☐

D Make sure all the guests' glasses are filled. ☐

E The rose has shed it's petals. ☐

F Amanda say's it's her's. ☐

G Angus says it's his. ☐

H It wasn't theirs; it was Toni and Jonie's. ☐

I Moses' toes are not roses. ☐

[5]

2 This passage has **ten** apostrophes used correctly and **ten** used incorrectly. Rewrite the passage, using apostrophes correctly.

When they were younger my grandparents' loved going to the movie's, although they called them the flicks or the picture's. Their town's local cinema was called the Paramount and was in the building that now house's Ronnie Renaldo's Discount Store. My granny's favourite films were musicals. She still likes Fred Astaire and Ginger Roger's, although she say's they we're a bit before her time, but the one she watches all the time is Gene Kelly's 'Singin' in the Rain'. She admires Kelly's dancing but she really prefers Donald O'Connor, especially the bit where he's having elocution lessons and sings a song about Moses'. Grandad disagree's but Granny says he doesn't know what he's talking about: he only ever watches babie's cartoons.

[20]

Total Marks _____ / 25

Punctuation

133

Punctuation

Inverted Commas 1: Quotations and Titles

1 Below is a short extract from *Romeo and Juliet* by William Shakespeare. Beneath it there is an extract from an essay, which quotes from the passage. None of the quotations have inverted commas (quotation marks) around them. Read both passages carefully and then insert inverted commas correctly in the second passage.

> O, she doth teach the torches to burn bright!
> It seems she hangs upon the cheek of night
> As a rich jewel in an Ethiop's ear –
> Beauty too rich for use, for earth too clear!
> So shows a snowy dove trooping with crows,
> As yonder lady o'er her fellow shows.

…A series of images emphasises how Juliet is superior to other women. She doth teach the torches to burn bright is an arresting visual image, especially if the stage is lit with torches. A rich jewel in an Ethiop's ear compares her to something precious and continues the idea of her as a bright light in the darkness. The contrast between light and darkness is continued with a snowy dove trooping with crows. At this point Romeo has not spoken to Juliet so everything he says is about her looks: beauty too rich for use. [4]

2 Tick the **five** sentences that are correctly punctuated.

- A   I think 'Romeo and Juliet' is my favourite play.
- B   When I was younger I liked 'Roald Dahl' books.
- C   I think the one I liked best was Matilda.
- D   My sister preferred 'James and the Giant Peach'.
- E   'A rose by any other name' is one of the world's best-known quotations.
- F   I think this means that 'everyone's the same' whatever they're called.
- G   My sister's name is 'Matilda', which I think is quite funny.'
- H   She says she's thinking of 'changing' her 'name'.
- I   'Romeo and Juliet' is about the Montagues and Capulets: 'two families both alike in dignity'.
- J   Shakespeare is sometimes referred to as 'the Bard'.

[5]

Total Marks _____ / 9

Workbook

Inverted Commas 2: Punctuating Speech

1 The passage below uses indirect (reported) speech to report a conversation. Rewrite it on a separate piece of paper using correctly punctuated direct speech.

Alex was getting fed up sitting at home all day, so she called her friend Daisy. Daisy said hello and Alex greeted her. Alex wondered if Daisy would like to meet her for a walk. Daisy replied that she would love to but her mum had grounded her until she had finished all her school work. Alex asked how long Daisy thought that would take. Daisy said that she would do it as fast as she could. The only problem was that she couldn't go too quickly because she might make careless errors. Her mother always checked her work and made her do it again if she thought it was not good enough. Alex commented that that must be an absolute nightmare. Her friend agreed but said she was hopeful that she might be finished in an hour or two and promised to call back as soon as she was free. [20]

2 Using direct speech, continue the conversation below. Aim for between 200 and 300 words.

> The two friends were walking home from school, when Harry stopped suddenly.
>
> 'Did you see what I just saw?' he asked.

[20]

Total Marks _____ / 40

Punctuation 135

Grammar

Nouns

1 This passage includes **ten** proper nouns but they have not been given capital letters. On a separate piece of paper, identify and list the proper nouns. Say which **two** of these are compound nouns.

It was my birthday on wednesday, 18th january. To celebrate, my mum and dad took me to nando's in marlborough street. They said I could invite two friends so I asked mark and louisa. Afterwards, I asked if they could come back to our house and dad said that would be fine. We watched a few videos, including 'the jungle book' (which mum loves and always sings along to) and 'frozen'. [12]

2 This passage from Rudyard Kipling's *The Jungle Book* describes the reaction of the monkeys to the arrival of the snake Kaa, as he comes to the rescue of the bear Baloo and the panther Bagheera. It includes **three** proper nouns (**one** repeated), **five** abstract nouns and **twelve** common nouns. Identify them and write them in the table below.

> Kaa was everything the monkeys feared in the jungle, for none of them knew the limits of his power, none of them could look him in the face, and none had ever come alive out of his hug. And so they ran, stammering with terror, to the walls and the roofs of the houses, and Baloo drew a deep breath of relief. His fur was much thicker than Bagheera's, but he had suffered sorely in the fight. Then Kaa opened his mouth for the first time and spoke…

Proper nouns	Abstract nouns	Common nouns

[20]

3 On a separate piece of paper, write a short, factual piece about your family, including at least **five** proper nouns, **two** abstract nouns, **three** collective nouns and **ten** common nouns. [20]

Total Marks _____ / 52

Workbook

Pronouns

1 The writer of the following paragraph has not used any pronouns. Replace the highlighted proper nouns and common nouns with pronouns in the spaces provided.

Hercules is known for Hercules' _____ enormous strength and the twelve 'Labours of Hercules', a series of seemingly impossible tasks which Hercules _____ was set. In a separate story, Hercules rescues Hesione, the daughter of the King of Troy. Hesione _____ has been tied to a rock, waiting to be eaten by a sea monster. The monster _____ is killed by Hercules. The King promises Hercules a reward but does not keep the king's _____ bargain. [5]

2 In the following passage identify **three** relative pronouns, **three** possessive pronouns, **two** personal pronouns, **one** reflexive pronoun and **one** emphatic pronoun. List them in the table below.

The story of Hercules, which I first heard in primary school, always intrigued me. I liked the idea of a hero who could overcome impossible odds. Hercules himself was not a conventional hero. In fact, he was not someone whom many people today would refer to as a 'role model'. In some ways he was his own worst enemy and did himself some damage. However, the gods loved him and, with their help, Hercules always found ways of completing his tasks successfully.

Relative	Possessive	Personal	Reflexive	Emphatic

[10]

3 Tick the **three** sentences in which the pronouns are used correctly.

A   We are both interested in mythology. ☐

B   The teacher lent me their book about Greek heroes. ☐

C   Mum asked me whose book it was. ☐

D   Myself and my brother have both read it. ☐

E   I blame myself for dropping it in the soup. ☐

F   My brother said that me and him were both to blame. ☐   [3]

Total Marks _____ / 18

Grammar

Grammar

Adjectives and Determiners

1 This extract includes **eight** adjectives and **four** different determiners.

a) List them in the table below the extract. If a word is repeated, list it only once.

> Then Kaa opened his mouth for the first time and spoke one long hissing word, and the far-away monkeys, hurrying to the defence of the Cold Lairs, stayed where they were, cowering till the loaded branches bent and crackled under them. The monkeys on the walls and the empty houses stopped their cries, and in the stillness that fell upon the city Mowgli heard Bagheera shaking his wet sides as he came from the tank.
>
> *The Jungle Book,* Rudyard Kipling

Adjectives	Determiners

[12]

b) Which **two** determiners could also be described as possessive pronouns?

_____ [2]

c) Which determiner indicates number? _____ [1]

2 This paragraph contains **ten** adjectives. Underline them. Then rewrite the paragraph replacing them to give the passage an atmosphere more appropriate to a horror or mystery story.

As the confident man emerged from the green woods, he noticed the blue skies and white clouds above him. In the distance was the tall tower he had read so much about. Its honey-coloured walls and shining windows gave it a friendly and welcoming air. He felt happy.

_____

_____

_____

_____

[20]

Total Marks _____ / 35

Workbook

Conjunctions

1 Insert 'and', 'but' or 'so' into the following sentences so that they make sense.

   a) Today I will be tidying up the garden _____ planting some seeds.

   b) It is not a large garden _____ it is big enough for us.

   c) I had a lot of things to move _____ I got out the wheelbarrow. [3]

2 Add 'either…or', 'neither…nor' or 'both…and' to the following sentences so that they make sense.

   a) We've had _____ the swing _____ the slide for years.

   b) _____ tidy the garden _____ go to the shops: it's your choice.

   c) _____ my brother _____ I like pears. [3]

3 Most of following sentences contain the same main clause but each has a different subordinating conjunction. Complete the sentences so that they make sense.

   a) We moved house because _____.

   b) We moved house despite _____.

   c) Although _____, we moved house.

   d) After _____, we moved house.

   e) We moved house in order to _____.

   f) We moved house before _____.

   g) We moved house whereas _____.

   h) While _____, we moved house. [8]

4 The following paragraph includes **two** coordinating conjunctions (**one** used twice) and **three** subordinating conjunctions. Circle the coordinating conjunctions and underline the subordinating conjunctions.

Although it was hard work, we enjoyed tidying up the garden. We filled the wheelbarrow with weeds, dead branches and other debris. After we had finished, we sat in the kitchen and talked about what we should do next. My brother was keen to get rid of the slide but I disagreed because I thought it could be mended. [5]

Total Marks _____ / 19

Grammar

Grammar

Verbs 1: Tenses

1 The following paragraph is written in the present tense, using the simple present and present continuous tenses. Rewrite it in the past tense, using both simple past and past continuous.

Macbeth is a soldier in the army of King Duncan. One day, while he is crossing a heath with his comrade Banquo, they are greeted by a strange apparition. They see three weird women, whom they take to be witches. The witches make a number of prophecies about Macbeth's future. They tell him he will be king. Banquo, noticing that they are prophesying great things for his friend, asks if they have a prophecy for him.

[11]

2 In the following passage **ten** verbs in the past tense have been incorrectly formed. Underline them and then write out the correct forms below.

For a long time the people of Scotland had knew that Macbeth was a tyrant. People heared stories about his evil deeds and some even seen omens of worse to come. When Lady Macduff and her children was murdered, Macduff weeped for them and for his country. He had went to England, where he have found Malcolm, Duncan's son. Malcolm persuaded Macduff to take revenge. He had already spoke to the King of England, who give him help and encouragement. Together they overthrowed the tyrant Macbeth.

[20]

Total Marks / 31

Workbook

Verbs 2

1 The following verbs can be used either transitive or intransitive. Show that you understand the difference by using each one twice, once as a transitive verb and once as an intransitive verb. For example, the verb 'drive' is transitive in 'I drive a car.' and intransitive in 'I am driving to town.'

a) clean

   i) Transitive _____

   ii) Intransitive _____

b) sing

   i) Transitive _____

   ii) Intransitive _____

[4]

2 Write a short paragraph (50–100 words) using the active voice to inform somebody about your favourite subject at school.

[10]

3 Rewrite each of these questions using a different modal verb to make them more polite.

a) Will you do the dishes? _____

b) Can I go now? _____ [2]

Total Marks _____ / 16

Grammar

Adverbs

1 Read this extract from *Her Benny* by Silas K Hocking, published in 1890, and answer the questions below. Benny and his younger sister have decided to run away from their cruel father and stepmother.

> Next morning Benny was stirring early, and when the first faint rays of the coming day peeped through the dust-begrimed and patched-up window, they saw the little fellow busily engaged in gathering together what things he and Nelly possessed previous to their final departure from home.
>
> Nelly still slept on, and several times the brother paused and looked fondly down upon the fair face of the sleeping child.

a) Find and write down **two** adverbs of manner (adverbs that show how something is done).

_____ [2]

b) Find and write down **two** adverbs of time (showing when something is done).

_____ [2]

c) Find and write down **two** adverbial phrases of time.

_____

_____ [2]

d) Find and write down an adverbial phrase indicating frequency (how often).

_____ [1]

e) Find and write down an adverbial subordinate clause.

_____

_____ [1]

f) Which of the above adverbial phrases could be described both as a fronted adverbial and a discourse marker?

_____ [1]

g) This extract comes at the beginning of a chapter. What does the opening discourse marker, 'next morning', tell you about the previous chapter?

_____ [1]

Total Marks _____ / 10

Workbook

Prepositions and Interjections

1 Read this extract from *Her Benny* by Silas K Hocking.

> Then he set to work again turning over a heap of rubbish that had been pushed as far back as possible under the stairs. At length a joyful exclamation burst from his lips as he came upon a small heap of potatoes.

Find and write down **five** prepositions.

....

.... [5]

2 Write **five** sentences of your own, using the prepositions you have identified above. Use a different preposition in each sentence.

a) ....

b) ....

c) ....

d) ....

e) .... [5]

3 Insert the most appropriate preposition in the following sentences. Choose from:

        by   to   with   into

        for   in   about

a) We were delighted .... the outcome of the match.

b) I was very surprised .... your reaction.

c) I'm very grateful .... your gift.

d) Can you give me an answer .... the question?

e) I've got no interest .... what happens next. [5]

4 Circle or underline the interjection in the following sentences / pairs of sentences.

a) Yes, of course I'll help you.

b) Oh my word! Did that really just happen?

c) The only answer I got was, 'Hrrmph!'

d) Great. I'll get on with it then. [4]

Total Marks .... / 19

Grammar

Grammar

Sentence Structure 1

1 The 'sentence' below is actually a fragment or minor sentence because it does not contain a verb.

Yesterday at noon

a) Using the fragment as a fronted adverbial, add a subject and verb to turn it into a simple sentence.

Yesterday at noon _____. [2]

b) Now add an object, either direct or indirect, with a preposition.

Yesterday at noon _____. [2]

c) Add **two** more words (either **two** adjectives or an adjective and an adverb) to give more detail.

Yesterday at noon _____. [2]

d) If your sentence is in the active voice, change it to the passive voice. If it is in the passive voice, change it to the active voice.

Yesterday at noon _____. [2]

2 Here is an example of the kind of sentence you might have ended up with:

Yesterday at noon, an elderly elephant sang a happy song and danced in the sunlit forest.

a) What is the subject of the first clause? _____

b) What is the verb in the first clause? _____

c) What is the object of the first clause? _____

d) Is it a direct or an indirect object? _____

e) Which word is the conjunction? _____

f) What is the subject of the second clause? _____

g) What is the verb in the second clause? _____

h) What is the indirect object of the second clause? _____

i) There are **two** prepositions in the sentence. What are they? _____

j) Is the sentence in the active or passive voice? _____ [10]

Total Marks _____ / 18

Workbook

Sentence Structure 2

1 Write **five** complex sentences about anything you like, each using a subordinating conjunction to show the appropriate relationship between the main and the subordinate clauses. For example, to show concession you might write:

The elephant was dancing although she felt sad.

a) Cause

b) Time

c) Place

d) Condition

e) Concession

[5]

2 Now write an original paragraph that includes a variety of sentence structures (up to **five** sentences), including at least **two** complex sentences.

[10]

Total Marks _____ / 15

Grammar

Grammar

Text Structure: Paragraphs

1 Arrange the following paragraphs in the correct order so that the whole passage makes sense. The text is a letter addressed to a local MP or councillor.

a) In addition, people returning home from the bars walk down our street on their way to the railway station. The station has been there since the mid-nineteenth century and its presence has never caused any problems before. Now, however, we are all too often disturbed by noisy late-night revellers, who not only sing and shout at the top of their voices but leave mounds of litter, including discarded takeaways and empty cans, behind them.

b) On behalf of the residents of Demerara Street, I would like to express our concern about the recent increase in anti-social behaviour in and around our street. Demerara Street was a quiet suburban street but has recently been turned into an unpleasant and potentially dangerous place to live.

c) We believe that there are several reasons for this. One is the opening of a new supermarket and several new bars on Main Street. Although they may be good for the local economy, they have attracted a lot of people from outside the area. Because of restricted and limited parking on Main Street, many customers park in Demerara Street, often illegally on the pavements, making life difficult for the residents, especially those with wheelchairs and prams.

d) Unlike the council, we do not mind 'doing our bit' to improve our street but we can only deal with the results of the anti-social behaviour. You, on the other hand, could deal with its causes. You might start by dealing with illegal parking in the street, liaising with the supermarket about improving its parking, and taking action to limit the numbers of bars and takeaways in the area.

e) This increase in litter is apparently of no concern to the council. We have never seen any attempt by council officials to deal with it despite many complaints. We have been forced to organise our own team of volunteers to clear up the mess, with no support or encouragement from the council.

[5]

2 From the passage above, identify the **four** discourse markers used to connect the paragraphs.

a) _____

b) _____

c) _____

d) _____

[4]

Workbook

3 What is the purpose of the final paragraph?

.... [1]

4 Write an article suitable for a newspaper or magazine with one of the following titles:

- Our Street
- My Tips for Stress-free Revision
- My Local Hero
- Do We Really Need Schools?
- Things Will Never Be the Same Again

Aim to write **five** paragraphs. Use discourse markers to make your article easy to follow. Continue on a separate piece of paper.

[10]

Total Marks .... / 20

Grammar

Standard English

1) Read through the piece you wrote in answer to Question 4 on page 147. Answer these questions.

   a) Have you tried to write mostly or entirely in Standard English? Yes / No

   b) If you have written mostly in Standard English, explain why you have done so.

   c) If all or part of your article is not in Standard English, explain why.

   d) Check to see if there are any places where you should have used Standard English words or phrases but have not. Make a note of these.

   e) Using the Revision Guide to help you, write down the Standard English versions of these words and phrases.

2 Write a first-person narrative called 'A Strange Incident', using a narrator who does not use Standard English.

3 Rewrite the same narrative, this time using a narrator from a different background, who does use Standard English.

10-Minute Spelling, Punctuation and Grammar Tests

Test 1

1 Which **two** of the following words are spelt correctly?

　A deceive ☐　　B recieve ☐　　C perceeve ☐　　D achieve ☐　　[2]

2 Which **two** of these sentences should end with a question mark?

　A When did Amil go to the shops ☐

　B Did Amil go to the shops ☐

　C I don't know whether Amil went to the shops ☐　　[2]

3 Which **two** of these words change their spelling when the suffix 'ful' is added?

　A success ☐　　B plenty ☐　　C fear ☐　　D mercy ☐　　[2]

4 In which of the following sentences are the commas used correctly?

　A Jana left the room and, went upstairs, ☐

　B After Jana had left the room, she went upstairs. ☐

　C Jana left the room, she went upstairs. ☐　　[1]

5 Insert brackets in the correct place in the following sentence.

　The cat a huge black and white creature hissed angrily.　　[2]

6 What does the colon introduce in this sentence?

　I ignored the cat's hissing: I was used to it.

　A a list ☐

　B a quotation ☐

　C an explanation ☐　　[1]

7 Underline the abstract noun in this sentence.

　He was an old cat but at the vet's he showed no fear.　　[1]

8 In what tense is this sentence written?

　On the way back he was purring contentedly.

　A past simple ☐　　B perfect ☐　　C past continuous ☐　　D past perfect ☐　　[1]

9 Which of these sentences uses the perfect tense correctly?

　A We have gave him his medication. ☐

　B We have give him his medication. ☐

　C We have given him his medication. ☐　　[1]

KS3 Spelling, Punctuation and Grammar Workbook

10 Underline the adverbial phrase in the following sentence.

The next day, he was back to normal. [1]

11 Which of these sentences is written in grammatically correct Standard English?

    A We was never taught painting at school. ☐

    B We were never taught painting at school. ☐

    C We were never teached painting at school. ☐ [1]

12 Which of the following examples of direct speech is correctly punctuated?

    A Maya said 'I would rather do pottery than painting.' ☐

    B 'I like painting Maya said but I prefer pottery.' ☐

    C 'I like painting,' Maya said, 'but I prefer pottery.' ☐ [1]

13 Which is the correct plural form of 'antiquity'?

    A antiquity's ☐

    B antiquitys ☐

    C antiquities ☐ [1]

14 In which of these sentences is the apostrophe used correctly?

    A I wouldn't like to be in your shoes. ☐

    B I would not like to be in your shoe's. ☐

    C I would'nt like to be in your shoes. ☐ [1]

15 Rewrite this sentence in the active voice.

All the toast was eaten by me. _____ [1]

16 Turn these **two** simple sentences into **one** complex sentence using a relative pronoun.

I saw Tom in the street. He is my cousin.

_____ [1]

Total Marks _____ / 20

10-Minute Spelling, Punctuation and Grammar Tests

Test 2

1 Which **two** of the following words are spelt correctly?

A regreted ☐   B regretted ☐   C benefited ☐   D benefitted ☐   [2]

2 What does the prefix 'post' mean in the words postnatal, postpone and posthumous?

A before ☐

B after ☐

C for ☐   [1]

3 Underline the subject of this sentence.

The car was buffeted by the wind.   [1]

4 Underline the adverb in this sentence.

However, we were relieved to get home.   [1]

5 In which **two** of these sentences is the comparative correct?

A The instructions seem more clearer now. ☐

B The instructions are much more clearer now. ☐

C The instructions seem clearer now. ☐

D I can see more clearly now. ☐   [2]

6 Underline the collective noun in this sentence.

In the distance the class could see hundreds of people.   [1]

7 Underline the subordinate clause in this sentence.

The people, who had come from the station, were on their way to the match.   [1]

8 Of what literary technique is the following phrase an example?

Old Father Time

A simile ☐   B oxymoron ☐   C personification ☐   D assonance ☐   [1]

9 Which of these sentences uses a semicolon correctly?

A Lisa likes; chips but Nat prefers mash. ☐

B Lisa likes chips; although Nat prefers mash. ☐

C Lisa likes chips; Nat prefers mash. ☐   [1]

KS3 Spelling, Punctuation and Grammar Workbook

10 Make this sentence less formal by rewriting it using **two** apostrophes for omission.

If you are there by eight, we will not be late.

_____ [2]

11 How many boys are there in this sentence?

The boy's boots are black.

A one ☐

B more than one ☐ [1]

12 Underline the main clause in this complex sentence.

Having left early, I had to wait for ages before I caught the train. [1]

13 Place **two** semicolons in the correct places in this sentence.

It was an amazing sight: piles of gold coins precious and semi-precious stones and a dazzling array of antique jewellery. [2]

14 Which **two** tenses are used in this sentence?

After Tom had finished his homework, he painted a picture.

A past continuous and perfect ☐

B simple past and perfect ☐

C simple past and past perfect ☐ [1]

15 Which of the following sentences is grammatically correct?

A Me and Nat was waiting for the train. ☐

B Nat and me were waiting for the train. ☐

C Nat and I were waiting for the train. ☐ [1]

16 Which of the following sentences is grammatically correct?

A If I was you, I would ask for a refund. ☐

B If I were you, I would ask for a refund. ☐

C If I were you, I will ask for a refund. ☐ [1]

Total Marks _____ / 20

10-Minute Spelling, Punctuation and Grammar Tests

Test 3

1 Which **two** of the following sentences are correct?

    A We're both in the basketball team.

    B I'm not sure were the match will be.

    C We have to wear our uniforms on the way there.

    D We we're top of the league a few weeks ago. [2]

2 Place a comma in the correct place in the following sentence.

    We had to travel by bus train and ferry to get there. [1]

3 What is the purpose of the ellipsis in this sentence? _____

    According to the poster, 'the shop will remain open…until further notice.' [1]

4 In which **two** of the following sentences are the apostrophes used correctly?

    A She's got a new bicycle.   C The bicycle's hers.

    B The bicycle is her's.   D She get's a new bicycle today. [2]

5 In which of the following sentences are inverted commas used correctly?

    A I'm reading 'Little Women by Louisa May Alcott'.

    B I'm reading 'Little Women' by Louisa May Alcott.

    C I'm reading Little Women by 'Louisa May Alcott'. [1]

6 Underline the noun phrase in this sentence.

    I think it was the best book I've ever read. [1]

7 In which **two** of these sentences is 'yourself' used correctly?

    A I'd like Rose and yourself to look after the hamster.

    B You yourself are responsible for that hamster.

    C Feed yourself before you feed the hamster. [2]

8 Which of the following sentences uses tenses correctly?

    A I knew that I have already read it.

    B I was knowing that I had alreadly read it.

    C I knew that I had already read it. [1]

9 Is the verb in this sentence transitive or intransitive?

I often read for pleasure. _____ [1]

10 Underline the preposition in this sentence.

I used to read to my little brother. [1]

11 Which of these sentences is written in Standard English?

A I would of gone if I'd known. ☐   C I would have went if I'd known. ☐

B I would of went if I'd knew. ☐   D I would have gone if I'd known. ☐ [1]

12 In which of these sentences is the word 'literally' used correctly?

A I'm so happy – I'm literally over the moon. ☐

B The house was literally fabulous. ☐

C I was so shocked that I was literally speechless. ☐ [1]

13 In this sentence to what does the participle clause 'sitting in the sun' refer?

Sitting in the sun, I noticed a woman feeding a dog.

A 'I' ☐   B 'a woman' ☐   C 'a dog' ☐   [1]

14 Which **two** of these words in the plural are spelt correctly?

A crisises ☐

B waltzs ☐

C antitheses ☐

D successes ☐ [2]

15 Which of these sentences is correctly punctuated?

A We decided, therefore, to stay in. ☐

B We had decided therefore we stayed in. ☐

C Therefore we decided, to stay in. ☐ [1]

16 Which of these words is an antonym of 'discrete'?

A indiscreet ☐   B combined ☐   C gossipy ☐   D separate ☐ [1]

Total Marks _____ / 20

10-Minute Spelling, Punctuation and Grammar Tests

Test 4

1 Which **two** of these words are spelt correctly?

    A playwrite ☐   **C** tragidy ☐

    B playwright ☐   **D** tragedy ☐   [2]

2 Which of these pairs of sentences is correctly spelt?

    A There boots are over their. They're the blue ones. ☐

    B They're boots are over here. Their the blue one. ☐

    C Their boots are over there. They're the blue ones. ☐   [1]

3 Which of these sentences could end with an exclamation mark?

    A Did you see what happened ☐   **C** I don't believe it ☐

    B I saw what happened ☐   [1]

4 Underline the common noun in this sentence.

Sophie feeds her pet rabbits every day.   [1]

5 Which of these sentences is written in Standard English?

    A Anna and I prefer those songs. ☐   **C** Me and Anna prefer those songs. ☐

    B Anna and I prefer them songs. ☐   **D** Me and Anna prefer them songs. ☐   [1]

6 Insert **two** dashes in the correct places in this sentence.

Con and Lia the girl next door were on the winning team.   [2]

7 Which **two** other forms of punctuation could you use instead of dashes in the sentence above? ....   [2]

8 Turn this sentence from the active to the passive voice.

The lion attacked the antelope.

....   [1]

9 What does the prefix 'circum' mean in the words 'circumnavigation' and 'circumference'?

    A beyond ☐   **C** around ☐

    B across ☐   **D** into ☐   [1]

10 Rewrite this sentence to show correctly punctuated direct speech.

I asked Do you like nature documentaries? Not really he replied.

_____ [1]

11 Which of the following sentences uses tenses correctly?

    A While I was waiting for the bus, the rain stopped. ☐

    B While I was waiting for the bus, the rain stops. ☐

    C While I waited for the bus, the rain has stopped. ☐ [1]

12 In which of these sentences are superlatives correctly used?

    A It's the most highest mountain in the range. ☐

    B It's the highest mountain in the range. ☐

    C It's the beautifulest view in the area. ☐ [1]

13 Which **two** of the following sentences are correctly expressed in Standard English?

    A I never done nowt. ☐   C I never did anything. ☐

    B I didn't do anything. ☐   D I ain't never done nothing. ☐ [2]

14 Which of these sentences uses a comparative adverb correctly?

    A You ran quicker than the others. ☐

    B You ran quicklier than the others. ☐

    C You ran more quickly than the others. ☐

    D You ran more quick than the others. ☐ [1]

15 Which of these is a minor sentence or fragment?

    A Zara lives. ☐   C Zara lives upstairs. ☐

    B Zara's upstairs. ☐   D Upstairs, Zara. ☐ [1]

16 Underline the subordinate clause in his sentence.

He locked the door every night before he went to bed. [1]

Total Marks _____ / 20

10-Minute Spelling, Punctuation and Grammar Tests

Test 5

1 Underline the adverb in this sentence.

We arrived early for our appointment. [1]

2 This sentence includes both a direct and an indirect object. Circle the direct object. Underline the indirect object.

He put the discarded packaging in the bin. [2]

3 Which of these sentences should end with a question mark?

A I will explain how to do it ☐

B It's not how it's done that's important, but why ☐

C How do they do that ☐ [1]

4 Which of these is the correct plural of 'monkey'?

A monkeys ☐ B monkies ☐ C monkey's ☐ [1]

5 Which **two** of the following sentences uses commas correctly?

A After doing her French revision, Rana had a break. ☐

B After, doing her French revision Rana had a break. ☐

C Rana did her French revision and, then she had a break. ☐

D Rana had done her French revision, so she had a break. ☐ [2]

6 Place a semicolon in the correct place in this sentence.

The leaves have turned brown the rain is falling. [1]

7 What does the prefix 'contra' mean in 'contradict' and 'contrary'?

A with ☐   C to ☐

B without ☐   D against ☐ [1]

8 Add **two** apostrophes in the correct places to this sentence.

Arthurs aunt says shes thinking of growing avocados. [2]

9 Which part of speech (word class) is the word 'weekly' in this sentence?

You will be paid on a weekly basis.

A verb ☐   C adverb ☐

B noun ☐   D adjective ☐ [1]

Workbook

10 What sort of sentence is this?

Tidy up before you leave.

A statement ☐   C exclamation ☐

B command ☐   D question ☐   [1]

11 Which of these sentences uses the past perfect tense correctly?

A I told her that we had tidied up. ☐   C I had told her we have tidied up. ☐

B I told her we have tidied up. ☐   D I had a good time tidying up. ☐   [1]

12 Underline the main clause in this complex sentence.

At the end of the day, the teacher told us that, if we wanted to, we could have a party on the last day of term.   [1]

13 Which of these sentences is written in grammatically correct Standard English?

A We were proper chuffed about the party. ☐

B We were real pleased about the party. ☐

C We were really pleased about the party. ☐

D We were made up about the party. ☐   [1]

14 Change these **two** simple sentences into **one** complex sentence using a relative pronoun.

Mr Beattie often pops in to see Mrs Rossini. Mr Beattie lives on the hill.

_____   [1]

15 Which **two** of the following words are spelt correctly?

A consciousness ☐   C consciense ☐

B conscientiously ☐   D conscicely ☐   [2]

16 Of what is the expression 'over the moon' an example in this sentence?

'I'm over the moon about having chips for tea.'

A metaphor and oxymoron ☐   C metaphor and hyperbole ☐

B personification and hyperbole ☐   D pathetic fallacy ☐   [1]

Total Marks _____ / 20

10-Minute Spelling, Punctuation and Grammar Tests

Test 6

1. Underline the determiner in this sentence.

   I'm hoping to get some bananas. [1]

2. Which of these sentences contains no spelling mistakes?

   A You've achieved a lot but your skating on thin ice now.

   B You've acheived a lot but you're skateing on thin ice now.

   C You've achieved a lot but you're skating on thin ice now.

   D You've achieved a lot but yore skateing on thin ice now. [1]

3. Which of these phrases is an oxymoron?

   A as cold as ice   B cold fire   C all fired up   D the ice age   [1]

4. Insert a comma and a full stop (followed by a capital letter) to create two sentences.

   My school bag is falling apart nevertheless I don't want a new one. [2]

5. What is a cliché? _____

   _____ [1]

6. Which of these sentences is written in grammatically correct Standard English?

   A The prisoner said they was innocent but pled guilty.

   B The prisoner said she was innocent but pleaded guilty.

   C The prisoner said she were innocent but pled guilty.

   D The prisoner said they were innocent but pleaded guilty. [1]

7. Which part of speech (word class) is the word 'well' in this sentence?

   Well, you could have knocked me down with a feather. _____ [1]

8. In this sentence there should be a punctuation mark between 'shade' and 'Bee'.

   Lee likes to sit in the shade Bee likes to lie in the sun.

   Which of these punctuation marks should **not** be used?

   A a full stop   B a comma   C a semicolon   D a dash   [1]

Workbook

9 Which of these nouns changes in the plural?

A woman ☐

B aircraft ☐

C sheep ☐ [1]

10 Which **two** of the following sentences are grammatically correct?

A Rain and snow is falling in York. ☐   C Rain and snow has fallen in York. ☐

B Rain and snow are falling in York. ☐   D Rain and snow have fallen in York. ☐ [2]

11 The following sentence contains both a coordinating conjunction and a subordinating conjunction. Circle the coordinating conjunction and underline the subordinating conjunction.

Although it was summer, the rain fell heavily and the wind blew fiercely, causing widespread damage. [2]

12 Which **two** of these sentences are written correctly?

A Who's project is this? ☐   C It belongs to Tom, who's sitting there. ☐

B I know whose it is. ☐   D Whose going to take it to him? ☐ [2]

13 Read this sentence:

The detective inferred that the solution was obvious.

Which of these sentences means the same thing?

A The detective hinted that the solution was obvious. ☐

B The detective deduced that the answer was self-evident. ☐

C The detective deduced that the formula was obvious. ☐

D The detective meant that the answer was obvious. ☐ [1]

14 Is the word 'criteria' singular or plural? _____ [1]

15 What is a topic sentence? _____

_____ [1]

16 Why are square brackets used in quotations? _____

_____ [1]

Total Marks _____ / 20

Spelling, Punctuation and Grammar Tests

Notes

Answers

Page 116: Vowels

1. a: android   b: bone   c: coin   d: declare
    e: educate   f: fright   g: gown   h: hound
    i: impure   j: jaunt   k: knight   l: lay
    m: mature   n: noon   p: pair   r: relay
    s: spare   t: toy   y: youth   z: zoology [20]

2.
ea	ee	ei	ie
defeat	indeed	ceiling	achieve
heave	preen	conceit	belief
knead	proceed	deceive	grieve
plead	sleeve	perceive	mischief
weaver	tweed	receipt	siege

    [20]

Page 117: Homophones

1. a) allusion – a passing reference; illusion – false belief / deceptive appearance
    b) alms – donation to the poor; arms – weapons / limbs
    c) aural – of hearing; oral – of speech
    d) bazaar – a sale or market; bizarre – strange [8]

2. a) buoy   b) mussels
    c) counsel   d) mousse
    e) waste   f) serial [6]

Page 118: Forming Plurals

1. a) alloys; authorities; blueberries; dairies; jockeys; monopolies; opportunities; quays [8]
    b) duchesses; glitches; impresarios; polishes; manifestos; mosquitoes; pagodas; stopwatches [8]
    c) crises; hippopotami (or hippopotamuses); indices (or indexes); knives; people (or persons); quizzes; soliloquies; strata [8]

2. children; fields; sheep; coats; boots; men; women; houses; tasks; dishes; floors; shoes; geese; offspring; patios; sandwiches; pizzas; tomatoes; boys; girls [20]

Page 119: Prefixes

1. auto——self; extra——beyond; inter——between; intra——within; mega——very big; post——after; pre——before; re——again; semi——half; sub——under; trans——across [11]

2. a) inter   b) post
    c) trans   d) pre
    e) sub   f) re
    g) auto   h) mega
    i) intra   j) semi
    k) extra [11]

Page 120: Suffixes

1.
Root Word	Present Participle	Past Participle
benefit	benefiting	benefited
delay	delaying	delayed
edit	editing	edited
imply	implying	implied
intensify	intensifying	intensified
regret	regretting	regretted
torpedo	torpedoing	torpedoed
underline	underlining	underlined

    [16]

2. a) parenthood   b) happiness
    c) elasticity   d) entirety [4]

3. a) competition   f) extortion
    b) reminiscence   g) identification
    c) remembrance   h) negligence
    d) prescription   i) deception
    e) commendation   j) remittance [10]

Page 121: Spelling Strategies

There are no set answers or marks for this page.

Page 122: Complex and Irregular Words

1. a) business   b) chronological
    c) conscience   d) exaggerate
    e) alliteration   f) development
    g) unfortunately [7]

2. a) queue   b) vicious
    c) consciousness   d) fulfilling
    e) Possession   f) discipline
    g) Onomatopoeia [7]

3. The correct spellings are:
    a) acknowledgment   acknowledgement
    b) auntie   aunty
    c) co-operative   cooperative
    d) dispatch   despatch
    e) focused   focussed
    f) homogenise   homgenize
    g) jail   gaol [7]

Page 123: Proofreading

1. baking; there; their; families; business; bakeries; benefiting; wholemeal; loaves; meringues [10]

2. thermometer; temperature; imaginary; emergency; required; immediate; fortunately; scissors; inoculation; fainted [10]

3. catering; agricultural; travelling; merchant; route; labourers; haymaking; outbuildings; pasture; poultry [10]

Page 124: Extending Your Vocabulary

1. There is no definitive answer. Examples might be: elderly; sauntering; unusual; cry; edged; disappeared; exhausted; bench; massive; oak [10]
2.
   a) agreement made by concession
   b) general agreement or opinion
   c) relating to existence
   d) dangerous
   e) obstacle [5]
3. role; principal; discreet; fewer; effect; complement; uninterested; infer; complacent; accept [10]

Page 125: Using Your Vocabulary Creatively 1

1. No set answers. [5]
2. No set answers. Examples of possible answers:
   a) Desperate Dan denies dastardly deeds
   b) Softly Sue slipped a slithery snake into the sandpit.
   c) Jody arrived like a thunderbolt.
   d) Fear stalked the city streets.
   e) Yusuf said that he was completely devastated and would never get over coming second. [5]

Page 126: Using Your Vocabulary Creatively 2

1. No set answer. [8, 2 marks for each language technique used effectively]

Page 127: Ending Sentences

1. a) . b) . c) ! (or .) d) ? e) .
   f) ? g) . (possibly !) h) . [8]
2. What is the point of exams? It's a subject everyone seems to have an opinion on. My English teacher thinks they're the only fair way of assessing progress but the music teacher disagrees. She believes in coursework. She thinks the exam boards should base their marks on the teachers' assessments. What if the teachers cheated by giving all their students top marks? She says it wouldn't happen. The English teacher says it happens all the time. Wow! I never thought I'd hear a teacher say that. [20]
3. The correct answers are: A and C. [2]

Pages 128–129: Commas

1. a) She told me she had visited Lanzarote, Tenerife, La Palma and Gran Canaria.
   b) She was so tired that, after she got home, she went straight to bed.
   c) In the morning, she phoned Bert, Lucy and me.
   d) She did not, however, speak to Pat.
   e) I said, 'Jan, how nice to hear from you.'
   f) Very kindly, she treated us all to a long, leisurely lunch.
   g) There was an amazing spread: chicken, ham, various salads and wonderful desserts.
   h) She said, 'I think Gran Canaria was my favourite, although I do love Tenerife.'
   i) I was torn between blackberry and apple pie, lemon and mango sorbet, and cheesecake.
   j) 'On the way back,' she said, 'I sat next to a really interesting person.' [20]
2. The correct answers are: A, C, D, F and H. [5]
3. Of course, when Pat returned, she too wanted to tell everyone about her holiday. She had been away longer than anyone else. She had been to Australia. She told us the reason she went there was that she had family out there. There was Uncle Barry, Aunty Beryl, Aunty Lynn, the newly weds Laurie and Jason, and lots of other cousins. She said she got on with all of them. They were really friendly. They welcomed her with open arms. Bert, who had been there, wondered if Pat would ever consider emigrating to Australia. She thought for a bit, then she said, 'No, I think I'd miss home too much.' I think she was waiting for someone to say we'd miss her. When nobody did, she looked a bit put out and ate her raspberry ripple in silence. [20]

Page 130: Colons, Semicolons, Hyphens and Slashes

1. a) Malcolm urges Macduff to avenge his family: 'Dispute it like a man.'
   b) There were five possible options: history, geography, RE, French and science.
   c) I have already read it; I'm sending it back.
   d) Gerry decided to buy the picture: it reminded him of home.
   e) The Vikings approached from the west; the Saxons came from the south. [5]
2. I noticed the advertisement at once: ' House contents for sale: bedroom furniture; all kitchen fittings; dining table and chairs; and a comfortable three-piece suite.' [5]
3. a) Any pupil needing a new bus pass should forward his / her details to the office.
   b) I've got boxes of what claimed to be non-stick pans.
   c) He came fully equipped with a fountain pen, a new ring-binder and plenty of paper.
   d) Sadly, 'all the kings horses and all the kings men / couldn't put Humpty together again.'
   e) Olivia Newton-John and John Travolta starred in 'Grease'. [5]
4. The correct answers are: A, B and E. [3]

Page 131: Parenthesis and Ellipsis

1. a) Constantine Rumbold (Con to his friends) lives in number 19.
   b) Number 21 (the big house with the bay windows) belongs to the Ahmed family.
   c) At the top of our street (Did I mention that I live there too?) is an empty property called The Birches.
   d) Mr and Mrs Allenby and their three children (Angus, Amanda and Ariadne) used to live there.
   e) Ariadne Allenby (18) is at university now. [5]
2. a) C: , the Allenbys' son, [1]
   b) B: their house [1]
   c) B: what would happen to the house [1]
   d) Angus Allenby – he's the boy I was telling you about – wrote to me about his new school. [2]

Page 132: The Apostrophe for Omission

1. **We're** all in this together. We **shouldn't** be standing on the sidelines watching **what's** happening from a distance. **It's** our future **they're** deciding on. **Let's** get in there and put our point of view. Maybe they **won't** listen. **That's** a chance we must take. One thing I can tell you: they **can't** listen if we **don't** say anything. [10]
2. The correct answers are: **C, D, E, F** and **G**. [5]

Page 133: The Apostrophe for Possession

1. The correct answers are: **C, D, G, H** and **I**. [5]
2. When they were younger my **grandparents** loved going to the **movies**, although they called them the flicks or the **pictures**. Their **town's** local cinema was called the Paramount and was in the building that now **houses** Ronnie **Renaldo's** Discount Store. My **granny's** favourite films were musicals. She still likes Fred Astaire and Ginger **Rogers**, although she **says** they **were** a bit before her time, but the one she watches all the time is Gene **Kelly's** 'Singin' in the Rain'. She admires **Kelly's** dancing but she really prefers Donald **O'Connor**, especially the bit where **he's** having elocution lessons and sings a song about **Moses**. Grandad **disagrees** but Granny says he **doesn't** know what **he's** talking about: he only ever watches **babies'** cartoons. [20]

Page 134: Inverted Commas 1: Quotations and Titles

1. …A series of images emphasises how Juliet is superior to other women. **'She doth teach the torches to burn bright'** is an arresting visual image, especially if the stage is lit with torches. **'A rich jewel in an Ethiop's ear'** compares her to something precious and continues the idea of her as a bright light in the darkness. The contrast between light and darkness is continued with **'a snowy dove trooping with crows'**. At this point Romeo has not spoken to Juliet so everything he says is about her looks: **'beauty too rich for use'**. [4]
2. The correct answers are: **A, D, E, I** and **J**. [5]

Page 135: Inverted Commas 2: Punctuating Speech

1. There is no definitive answer to this question. Award yourself **2 marks** for every statement or question that is in inverted commas, starts on a new line and is correctly punctuated. [20]
2. There is no definitive answer to this question. Award yourself **2 marks** for every statement or question that is in inverted commas, starts on a new line and is correctly punctuated. [20]

Page 136: Nouns

1. Wednesday; January; Nando's; Marlborough Street (compound); Mark; Louisa; Dad; 'The Jungle Book' (compound); Mum; 'Frozen' [12]

2.

Proper nouns	Abstract nouns	Common nouns
Kaa	limits	everything
Baloo	power	monkeys
Bagheera	terror	jungle
	relief	face
	time	hug
		walls
		roofs
		houses
		breath
		fur
		fight
		mouth

[20]

3. **1 mark** for each proper noun (five), abstract noun (two), collective noun (three) and common noun (ten) used appropriately. [20]

Page 137: Pronouns

1. his; he; she; it; his [5]
2.

Relative	Possessive	Personal	Reflexive	Emphatic
which	his	he	himself	himself
who	their	he		
whom	his			

[10]

3. The correct answers are: **A, C** and **E**. [3]

Page 138: Adjectives and Determiners

1. a)

Adjectives	Determiners
first	his
long	the
hissing	one
far-away	their
cold	
loaded	
empty	
wet	

[12]

b) 'his' and 'their' [2]

c) one [1]

2. The adjectives are: confident, green, blue, white, tall, honey-coloured, shining, friendly, welcoming and happy. **[20, 10 marks for 10 adjectives and 1 mark for every appropriate replacement adjective chosen]**

Page 139: Conjunctions

1. a) and, b) but, c) so [3]
2. a) both…and   b) Either…or   c) Neither…nor / Both…and [3]
3. There are no definitive answers to this question. Examples of suitable answers are:
   a) We moved house because we needed more room.
   b) We moved house despite being very happy there.
   c) Although we knew we would miss the neighbours, we moved house.
   d) After we left school, we moved house.
   e) We moved house in order to be nearer our grandparents.

f) We moved house before the new term started.
g) We moved house whereas the Parkers decided to stay.
h) While the weather was good, we moved house. [8]

4. Coordinating conjunctions: but, and. Subordinating conjunctions: Although, After, because. [5]

Page 140: Verbs 1: Tenses

1. Macbeth **was** a soldier in the army of King Duncan. One day, while **he was crossing** a heath with his comrade Banquo, they **were greeted** by a strange apparition. They **saw** three weird women, whom they **took** to be witches. The witches **made** a number of prophecies about Macbeth's future. They **told** him he **would** be king. Banquo, noticing that they **were** prophesying great things for his friend, **asked** if they **had** a prophecy for him. [11]

2. For a long time the people of Scotland had knew **had known** that Macbeth was a tyrant. People heared **heard** stories about his evil deeds and some even seen **saw** omens of worse to come. When Lady Macduff and her children was murdered **were murdered**, Macduff weeped **wept** for them and for his country. He had went **had gone** to England, where he have found **had found** Malcolm, Duncan's son. Malcolm persuaded Macduff to take revenge. He had already spoke **had already spoken** to the King of England, who give **gave** (or **had given**) him help and encouragement. Together they overthrowed **overthrew** the tyrant Macbeth. [20]

Page 141: Verbs 2

1. Possible answers include:
   a) i) I cleaned the bath.   ii) I cleaned for money.
   b) i) I sang a solo.   ii) I sang badly. [4]
2. Award yourself **1 mark** each time you successfully use an active verb. [10]
3. There are no definitive answers. Suggestions are:
   a) Would you do the dishes?
   b) May I go now? [2]

Page 142: Adverbs

1. a) 'busily' and 'fondly' [2]
   b) 'early' and 'still' [2]
   c) 'Next morning' and 'previous to their final departure from home' [2]
   d) 'several times' [1]
   e) 'when the first faint rays of the coming day peeped through the dust-begrimed and patched-up window' [1]
   f) Next morning [1]
   g) That the previous chapter took place the previous day [1]

Page 143: Prepositions and Interjections

1. to, over, under, from, of [5]
2. No definitive answers. Give yourself **1 mark** for each sentence in which a preposition is used appropriately. [5]

3. a) with ('by' and 'about' are also acceptable)
   b) by   c) for   d) to   e) in [5]
4. a) Yes   b) Oh my word   c) Hrrmph
   d) Great [4]

Page 144: Sentence Structure 1

1. There are no definitive answers. Examples of possible answers are:
   a) Yesterday at noon, an elephant sang. [2]
   b) Yesterday at noon, an elephant sang a song to me. [2]
   c) Yesterday at noon, an elderly elephant sang a happy song. [2]
   d) Yesterday at noon, a happy song was sung by an elderly elephant. [2]
2. a) an elderly elephant   b) sang
   c) a happy song   d) direct object
   e) and   f) an elderly elephant
   g) danced   h) the sunlit forest
   i) 'at' and 'in'   j) active [10]

Page 145: Sentence Structure 2

1. There are no definitive answers. Give yourself **1 mark** for each sentence that uses a conjunction effectively to introduce a subordinate clause. Examples of possible answers:
   a) The elephant was dancing because she was happy.
   b) The elephant was dancing after she had eaten.
   c) The elephant was dancing when she got to the clearing.
   d) The elephant was dancing until it started to get dark.
   e) The elephant was dancing despite the rain falling. [5]
2. Give yourself **2 marks** for each properly constructed and punctuated sentence. [10]

Pages 146–147: Text Structure: Paragraphs

1. The correct order is: b), c), a), e), d). [5]
2. a)–d): several reasons for this / In addition / This increase in litter / Unlike the council [4]
3. To make suggestions about how things can be changed. [1]
4. Give yourself **2 marks** for each effective paragraph. [10]

Pages 148–149: Standard English

There are no marks for these questions.

10-Minute Spelling, Punctuation and Grammar Tests

Pages 150–151: Test 1

1. A and D [2]
2. A and B [2]
3. B and D [2]
4. B [1]
5. The cat (a huge black and white creature) hissed angrily. [2]
6. C [1]
7. fear [1]

8.	C	[1]		7.	Commas and brackets	[2]
9.	C	[1]		8.	The antelope was attacked by the lion.	[1]
10.	The next day	[1]		9.	C	[1]
11.	B	[1]		10.	I asked, 'Do you like nature documentaries?' 'Not really,' he replied.	[1]
12.	C	[1]		11.	A	[1]
13.	C	[1]		12.	B	[1]
14.	A	[1]		13.	B and C	[2]
15.	I ate all the toast.	[1]		14.	C	[1]
16.	I saw Tom, who is my cousin, in the street.	[1]		15.	D	[1]
				16.	before he went to bed	[1]

Pages 152–153: Test 2

1. B and C [2]
2. B [1]
3. The car [1]
4. However [1]
5. C and D [2]
6. class [1]
7. who had come from the station [1]
8. C [1]
9. C [1]
10. If you're there by eight, we won't / we'll not be late. [2]
11. A [1]
12. I had to wait for ages [1]
13. It was an amazing sight: piles of gold coins; precious and semi-precious stones; and a dazzling array of antique jewellery. [2]
14. C [1]
15. C [1]
16. B [1]

Pages 154–155: Test 3

1. A and C [2]
2. We had to travel by bus, train and ferry to get there. [1]
3. To show that some words have been omitted. [1]
4. A and C [2]
5. B [1]
6. the best book I've ever read [1]
7. B and C [2]
8. C [1]
9. Intransitive [1]
10. the second 'to' [1]
11. D [1]
12. C [1]
13. A [1]
14. C and D [2]
15. A [1]
16. B [1]

Pages 156–157: Test 4

1. B and D [2]
2. C [1]
3. C [1]
4. rabbits [1]
5. A [1]
6. Con and Lia – the girl next door – were on the winning team. [2]

Pages 158–159: Test 5

1. early [1]
2. He put the discarded (packaging) in the bin. [2]
3. C [1]
4. A [1]
5. A and D [2]
6. The leaves have turned brown; the rain is falling. [1]
7. D [1]
8. Arthur's aunt says she's thinking of growing avocados. [2]
9. D [1]
10. B [1]
11. A [1]
12. the teacher told us [1]
13. C [1]
14. Mr Beattie, who lives on the hill, often pops in to see Mrs Rossini. [1]
15. A and B [2]
16. C [1]

Pages 160–161: Test 6

1. some [1]
2. C [1]
3. B [1]
4. My school bag is falling apart. Nevertheless, I don't want a new one. [2]
5. An overused word / phrase. [1]
6. B [1]
7. An interjection. [1]
8. B [1]
9. A [1]
10. B and D [2]
11. Although it was summer, the rain fell heavily (and) the wind blew fiercely, causing widespread damage. [2]
12. B and C [2]
13. B [1]
14. Plural [1]
15. A sentence at the beginning of a paragraph that introduces its subject. [1]
16. To show that the word / phrase within them is not in the original text. [1]

Acknowledgements

The author and publisher are grateful to the copyright holders for permission to use quoted materials and images. Every effort has been made to trace copyright holders and obtain their permission for the use of copyright material. The author and publisher will gladly receive information enabling them to rectify any error or omission in subsequent editions. All facts are correct at time of going to press.

Published by Collins
An imprint of HarperCollins*Publishers* Ltd
1 London Bridge Street
London SE1 9GF

HarperCollins*Publishers*
Macken House, 39/40 Mayor Street Upper,
Dublin 1, D01 C9W8, Ireland

© HarperCollins*Publishers* Limited 2021

ISBN 9780008470517

First published 2021

10 9 8 7

All rights reserved. No part of this publication may be reproduced, stored in a retrieval system, or transmitted, in any form or by any means, electronic, mechanical, photocopying, recording or otherwise, without the prior permission of Collins.

British Library Cataloguing in Publication Data.

A CIP record of this book is available from the British Library.

Commissioning: Katie Sergeant, Clare Souza and Richard Toms
Author: Paul Burns
Project Manager: Katie Galloway
Editor: Jill Laidlaw
Cover Design: Kevin Robbins and Sarah Duxbury
Inside Concept Design: Ian Wrigley
Typesetting and artwork: Jouve India Private Limited
Production: Karen Nulty
Printed in India by Multivista Global Pvt. Ltd.

MIX
Paper | Supporting responsible forestry
FSC™ C007454

This book is produced from independently certified FSC™ paper to ensure responsible forest management.

For more information visit: www.harpercollins.co.uk/green